THOUSAND OAKS LIBRARY

P9-CAA-880

NEWBURY PARK BRANCH

DISCARDED

Collection Management

| 8/01 - 2 (5/01) | | | |
| 12/14 | 23 | 6/14 | |

THOUSAND OAKS LIBRARY
1401 E. Janss Road
Thousand Oaks, CA 91362

Tales and Treasures of the
CALIFORNIA
GOLD RUSH

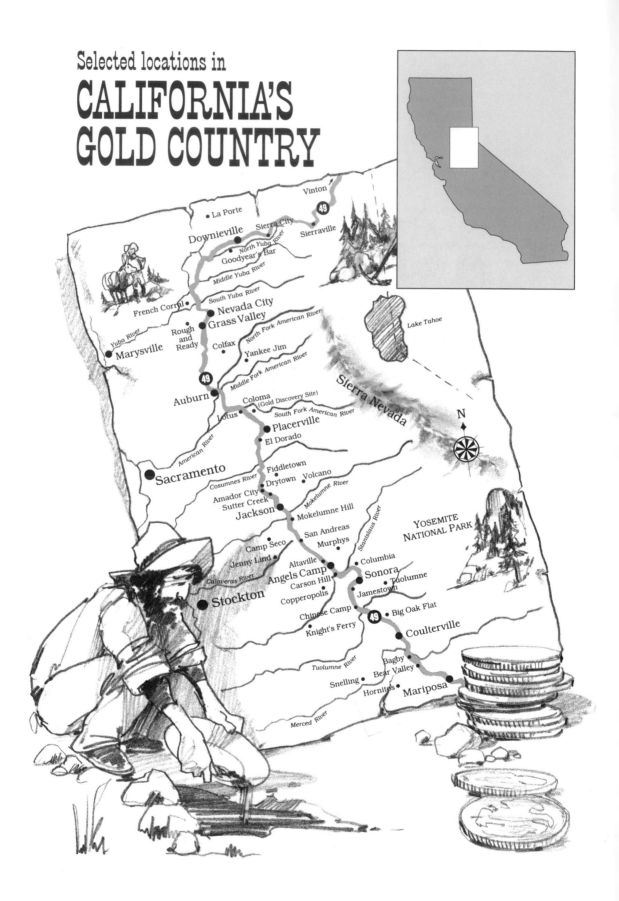

Selected locations in
CALIFORNIA'S
GOLD COUNTRY

Vinton
La Porte
Downieville · Sierra City
Sierraville
North Yuba River
Goodyear's Bar
Middle Yuba River
South Yuba River
French Corral
Nevada City
Grass Valley
Lake Tahoe
Yuba River
Rough and Ready
Colfax
North Fork American River
Marysville
Yankee Jim
Middle Fork American River
Sierra Nevada
Auburn
Coloma
(Gold Discovery Site)
South Fork American River
Lotus
Placerville
American River
El Dorado
Sacramento
Fiddletown
Cosumnes River
Drytown
Volcano
Amador City
Mokelumne River
Sutter Creek
Jackson
Mokelumne Hill
YOSEMITE
NATIONAL PARK
San Andreas
Camp Seco
Murphys
Stanislaus River
Jenny Lind
Altaville
Columbia
Calaveras River
Angels Camp
Sonora
Carson Hill
Tuolumne
Stockton
Copperopolis
Jamestown
Chinese Camp
Big Oak Flat
Knight's Ferry
Coulterville
Tuolumne River
Bagby
Bear Valley
Snelling
Hornitos
Mariposa
Merced River

N

Tales and Treasures of the
CALIFORNIA GOLD RUSH

Randall A. Reinstedt

Illustrated by Ed Greco

Ghost Town Publications
Carmel, California

Randall A. Reinstedt's
History & Happenings of California Series
Ghost Town Publications
P.O. Drawer 5998
Carmel, CA 93921

10 9 8 7 6 5 4

© 1994 by Randall A. Reinstedt
All rights reserved. No part of this publication may be reproduced,
stored in a retrieval system, or transmitted in any form or by any means,
electronic, mechanical, photocopying, recording, or otherwise, without
prior written permission of the publisher.

Manufactured in the United States of America

Library of Congress Catalog Number 94-76792
ISBN 0-933818-28-9 Hardcover
ISBN 0-933818-80-7 Softcover

Edited by John Bergez
Cover design and illustrations by Ed Greco
Typesetting by Erick and Mary Ann Reinstedt

J979.404

CONTENTS

The tale of the Lake of Gold excited miners from miles around (see Chapter 7).

INTRODUCTION

I have always been fascinated by the people, places, and events connected with the fabulous California Gold Rush. For many years I have been collecting information and stories about that exciting and colorful time. I wrote this book to share some of my favorite tales with you.

A number of these stories are about treasures—buried treasures, treasures hidden in all kinds of places and containers, and even lost outlaw loot! As you will see, California's Gold Country is rich in tales of gold and other valuables that were stashed away by their owners, only to be lost or forgotten. Many of these missing treasures may still be there today, waiting for some lucky person to find them!

Of course, the word "treasure" means different things to different people. One person might imagine a chest brimming with golden nuggets, while another would be happy to find a rusty tin can with a few old coins inside. The fabled treasures of the Gold Country include both of these types of lost riches, as well as many others that fall somewhere in between.

As for me, my own treasure hunts are a bit different than most. Instead of digging in the ground, I "dig" through books and magazines, as well as aged newspapers, letters, and diaries. Instead of tracking down buried stores of wealth, I go looking for old-timers who have memories to share of days gone by.

You see, I find my "treasures" in stories of the way things used to be. What was it like for the Forty-Niners to come to California from across the country, or halfway around the world? What did they do when they got to the gold fields? What stories are behind some of the strange names they gave to the mining camps—names like Hangtown, Sorefinger, and Yankee Jim?

And what about the outlaws who prowled the Sierras? Who was the famous stagecoach robber Black Bart, and what happened to him? How did badman Tom Bell get started on his life of crime? When he was captured for the last time, what were his parting words before he was hanged?

In the chapters to come, questions like these will be the "treasure map" that takes us back through time to the rough and ready days of the Gold Rush. At the end of the trail, we will meet the hardy miners of the Sierra Nevada, digging (and sometimes fighting) for their hard-won gold . . . playing cards (and practical jokes) to pass the time . . . handing out rough justice to those who break the rules . . . and showering gold coins on Little Lotta, the singing and dancing "child star" who captured their hearts.

Along the way, we will hear tales of the lucky few who stumbled upon instant riches in the strangest ways. But we'll also learn about some of the unlucky ones who never got to reclaim their hidden treasures—sometimes because they were killed for them first!

It is stories like these that bring the Gold Rush back to life. I have had a lot of fun "digging up" these tales and retelling them for you. Perhaps they will start you on your own treasure hunt into the past. You might begin by doing some digging in your local library. Better yet, try tracking down an old-timer or two in your family or community, and ask them to tell you their own stories of days gone by.

Remember, there are fascinating tales to be discovered about every time and place—not just the Sierra Nevada of Gold Rush days. Even if you never come across a chest full of gold, you *can* uncover countless treasures of the past, beginning in your own backyard!

Happy hunting!

GOLD!

Who Found the Gold?

When was gold discovered in California? And who found it?

If you're like most people, you probably think of the year 1848 as the "official" start of California's famed Gold Rush. It was in January of that year that James Wilson Marshall found gold along the western slope of the Sierra Nevada, in northern California. After Marshall's discovery, California would never be the same.

But was James Marshall the *first* person to glimpse the hidden treasures of the Golden State? To answer this question, let's travel back in time about six years before the Marshall find, and hundreds of miles to the south.

It is the year 1842, and a man named Francisco Lopez is gathering wild onions in rugged Placerita Canyon in Los Angeles County. Like Marshall, Lopez isn't looking for gold. So you can imagine his surprise when he sees flakes of yellow clinging to the roots of some of his onions! As he carefully brushes the little flakes into his palm, the amazing truth dawns on him. The yellow metal is gold!

Lopez's eyes must have shone with delight. It was as if you were out in the country collecting rocks and found bits of treasure hiding underneath!

Lopez's discovery didn't cause hordes of fortune seekers to set out for California, but it did create a flurry of excitement. In fact, gold from the Placerita Canyon region was sent to the United States Mint in Philadelphia for several years. So perhaps it is the little-known Francisco Lopez who deserves the honor of starting California's "golden history."

Although Lopez's find may have been the earliest sizable strike in California, *talk* of gold goes back even farther in time. An interesting example takes us to the Santa Lucia Mountains in central California. The story involves a Scotsman named David Douglas, who later became a world-famous botanist (someone who studies plant life). In 1833, the story goes, Douglas was roaming the coastal mountain range when he found gold in the roots of a great tree!

Douglas's discovery didn't make him famous, but his work as a botanist did. In fact, the beautiful Douglas fir tree is named after him.

About eight years before the Douglas incident, the famed mountain man Jedediah Strong Smith got into the act. In 1825, he and his band of fur trappers reportedly found gold near Mono Lake, on the east side of the Sierra mountains.

Backing up still further, talk of California gold includes tales of mission treasures and "Lost Padre" mines. Historians disagree about the truth of these stories, but such tales could mean that the Spanish knew about California's buried wealth long before the Marshall find.

The famed English seafarer Francis Drake should also be included in this account. During his famous voyage around the world in 1577–1580, Drake spent time on the central California coast. In written records made after the voyage,

10

there are hints that he or his men found evidence of both gold and silver in the area around San Francisco Bay—more than 250 years before the Gold Rush got its start!

So who was the *first* to discover California's gold? Probably the best answer is the *first* people who populated the land—the California Indians. No doubt many of these native Californians came across the pockets of glitter and veins of yellow ore that later caused the largest gold rush the world has ever seen. But unlike future fortune hunters, California's first people were never swept up in "gold fever," and their discoveries went largely unrecorded. So it is that the name of the *true* discoverer of California's gold will remain forever a mystery.

James Marshall's Lucky Find—Or Was It?

For most people, the start of California's Gold Rush dates back to the famous find by James Wilson Marshall on January 24, 1848. Both Marshall and John Augustus Sutter, the founder of nearby Sutter's Fort, will always be linked with the story of the Gold Rush. But for these two men, the discovery of gold wasn't the lucky strike you might imagine.

Marshall's discovery happened in an area known to the local Indians as Cul-huh-mah (meaning "beautiful valley"). Today we call it Coloma.

The South Fork of the American River flows through the valley and adds to its beauty. This Sierra Nevada stream played an important part in Marshall's discovery. The

gold he found on that January morning was in a canal that his men had dug near the river.

The water that flowed through the canal was diverted from the South Fork and acted as a power source to turn a large paddlewheel. The paddlewheel was attached to machinery in a sawmill that Marshall's crew of carpenters were building. The machinery powered saws for cutting wood that was brought to the mill from nearby forests. Later the men planned to use the river to transport the lumber to a location near Sutter's Fort.

Despite its name, Sutter's Fort was not actually a military fort. Instead, it was the home and headquarters of John Sutter. It *looked* like a fort, however, because it had a high wall around it, complete with cannons at the corners and entrance. People who visited there began calling the place Sutter's Fort, and the name stuck. Perhaps it was a fitting name, because Indians once told Sutter that the cannons kept them from attacking the complex.

It was Sutter who hired James Marshall to build the sawmill. Some people say that he planned to use the wood from Marshall's mill to build a town that was to be called Sutterville. Whatever Sutter's ideas were, they were changed forever when news of Marshall's discovery began history's greatest gold rush!

The Gold Rush made both Marshall and Sutter very famous. Most people probably imagine that they also became very rich and lived happily ever after. However, fate had other plans in store.

Sadly, James Marshall's last few years were spent in poverty. His "lucky" find made many other people wealthy, but

Marshall himself was forced to live off handouts, handyman jobs, and the small amounts of money he could earn from selling his autograph.

As for John Sutter, this remarkable man of courage and foresight helped many early settlers get their start in California. But after a series of ups and downs, he too was anything but rich in his later years. When he died in a small town in Pennsylvania, the famous founder of Sutter's Fort was nearly penniless.

By the way, there is more than one story about who actually found the gold near Marshall's sawmill. Some sources say that it was one of the men who was helping to build the sawmill, and not Marshall himself.

But my favorite tale states that the real heroes were two boys and a girl whose parents worked at the mill. The children found some yellow metal, which they showed to their mother (who worked as a cook). It was only then that Marshall got wind of the gold that was lying practically under his feet.

Whether this account is true, I can't say. But it *is* fun to think that the famous Marshall discovery was actually made by three young people like yourself—young people who helped to change the history of the Golden State, and of the world!

Who Started the Gold Rush?

Regardless of who actually found the first gold near the South Fork of the American River, James Marshall and John Sutter certainly get a lot of the credit for the historic discovery. But who really started the Gold Rush? Was it Marshall, who may have found the yellow metal? Was it Sutter, the man he worked for? Or was it a third man, somebody many people have never heard of?

The man I'm thinking of was named Samuel Brannan. Brannan arrived in California in 1846. Marshall's find was still two years in the future, and there was little talk of gold when Brannan settled in the small village of Yerba Buena, on San Francisco Bay. While he was there, he acquired land and started businesses. Among his businesses was a newspaper called the *California Star*. Brannan used the paper for advertising and to report newsworthy events.

At that time Sutter's Fort was a popular stopping-off place for overland settlers arriving in California. Brannan and a partner decided to open a store outside the walls of Sutter's complex. The store stocked such things as hardware, dry goods, liquor, and general merchandise.

One day in 1848, a wagon driver tried to pay for some liquor at the store with a gold nugget. The nugget had come from the site of Marshall's sawmill. It was in this way that Brannan learned about the gold discovery.

Sutter and Marshall wanted to keep the find a secret, but the excited Brannan had other ideas. He knew that once the word got out, people from far and near would flock to the area. He would never again have to worry about having enough customers for his store!

Cleverly, Brannan stocked up on merchandise that the miners would need. The next step was to make sure that people heard about the riches waiting to be found near Sutter's Fort.

Brannan knew just what to do. First he went to Coloma and put some gold in a bottle. His next stop was San Francisco (which had recently changed its name from Yerba Buena). Running up and down the streets, he waved his bottle and shouted "Gold! Gold from the American River!" Stopping at the little town's busy Portsmouth Square, he showed off the bottle of gold to the people who had gathered there.

Many of the townsfolk had heard rumors of gold in the Sierras, but they didn't believe them. Now, seeing the gold and

talking to Brannan, they were convinced. The rumors were true!

Making good use of his newspaper, Brannan had special copies printed telling about the gold. Some of his newspapers found their way to a ship that was about to sail for the Atlantic coast. It is not difficult to imagine the excitement these papers created when they reached the East.

Just as Brannan expected, gold seekers were soon flocking to Sutter's Fort, Coloma, and the hills and canyons of the Sierras. Before long, whole towns emptied as men left their jobs to set out for the gold fields.

The rush for gold was on! And even though James Marshall may have found the gold, you could say that it was Sam Brannan who started the Gold Rush!

2 CALIFORNIA, HERE I COME!

Where Did Everybody Come From?

By 1849 news of the great gold discovery was spreading from person to person, town to town, state to state, and nation to nation. So was gold fever! All around the globe, people dropped what they were doing and headed for California. Most of the argonauts (gold seekers) were from the United States, but others came from such places as Mexico, South America, Hawaii, China, Spain, Germany, France, Holland, and England.

The majority of the fortune hunters from other lands traveled by sea to San Francisco and then made their way to the gold fields. With so many newcomers passing through, the tiny port city experienced a remarkable change. In a surprisingly short time it grew from a sleepy bayside village to one of the busiest towns in the territory.

How fast did San Francisco grow? Before the Gold Rush its entire population of fewer than 1,000 people would have fit comfortably in a modern school gym. By the end of 1849, nearly 25,000 people called the bay city home! Besides all these newcomers who lived and worked in the bustling community, there were countless others who passed through the town on their way to the gold fields.

For the next leg of their journey the gold seekers boarded another boat for a trip up the Sacramento River. Many of these vessels tied up along the river bank near Sutter's Fort. From there the argonauts made their way overland to the mining camps.

Before long a town began to grow up along the river. Like San Francisco, it later became a large and beautiful city that has played an important part in the history of our state. Today we know it as Sacramento—the capital of California!

Most of the Americans who traveled to California by sea went by one of two ways. For those who left from the East Coast, the most popular route was around South America's rugged and dangerous Cape Horn. The rough weather and water around the Horn sent many ships and passengers to their graves. If the argonauts were lucky, they made it to California in six months.

The second sea route was shorter and took only about four months if things worked out. But this trip was also more expensive. Actually, those who took this route did not travel all the way by water. Instead of rounding Cape Horn, their vessels passed through the Caribbean Sea and headed for the east coast of Panama, in Central America. After the ships dropped anchor near the mouth of the Chagres River, the gold seekers were faced with making their way across the Isthmus of Panama.

The Isthmus is a narrow strip of land that connects North and South America. Today ships cross the Isthmus through the Panama Canal, but in Gold Rush days, there was no way for ships to get across. Most of the argonauts hired native guides to take them up rivers, across mountains, and through the beautiful—but dangerous—jungles and swamps of Panama.

When they finally reached the Pacific Coast, the weary travelers had to wait for a second vessel to take them north to California. Often they had to wait for many weeks—sometimes for months. At times there were as many as 2,000 people waiting anxiously for a ship!

One of the reasons for the long wait was the glut of vessels that filled San Francisco Bay. Like everyone else, their crews had been bitten by the gold bug. When ships arrived at the busy port city, sailors by the hundreds gave up their jobs and ran off for the gold fields. At one time, some 500 vessels were stranded in the bay!

The abandoned ships crowding the harbor must have been quite a sight. They probably gave off an impressive smell, too. Many of their cargos rotted because no one could be found to unload them. In time the hulks of some of these vessels took on a new life and became almost a part of the city. They were used as hotels, restaurants, lodging houses, and saloons. To this day, ships from the time of the Gold Rush lie buried under the streets and buildings of San Francisco.

In addition to the gold seekers who traveled to California by sea, thousands of Americans went by land. This was the least expensive way, but it took even more courage than the risky sea routes. Many people set out from the communities of St. Joseph and Independence, in the state of Missouri. Ahead of them lay nearly 2,000 miles of plains, mountains, rivers, and desert. For them, the quest for gold meant six agonizing months of hardships and heartache.

But danger and discomfort didn't discourage the argonauts. By sea and by land, they continued to come. According to one source, by 1850 there were 125,000 people living in California (other sources say the number was even greater). And about 8 out of every 10 of these Californians arrived during the Gold Rush!

Where Did Everybody Go?

Many of the first fortune hunters to arrive in California headed for the area around Sutter's Fort. Few of them stayed very long. After buying supplies and questioning other gold seekers about the latest strikes, they headed for the "diggings."

From Sutter's Fort, some argonauts went north and some went south, while others chose to try their luck in the nearby mountains and streams. Gold Country gossip and rumors of new discoveries often helped decide their course.

The story was the same in other gateway communities, like the San Joaquin River town of Stockton. Thousands of argonauts passed through, but few lingered long enough to plant their roots or call the towns home.

After Marshall's famous find at Sutter's mill in 1848, gold was found at several other locations along the western slope of the Sierras. By the time the hordes of gold hunters began arriving the following year, one of the many problems they faced was deciding where to dig. These gold seekers, of course, were called Forty-Niners, because they came to California in 1849. Today this name is well known, and not just in connection with the Gold Rush. The San Francisco 49ers professional football team has added its own brand of magic to the name.

But in 1849 the magic word was "gold"! Wave after wave of Forty-Niners poured into the Gold Country. An estimated 35,000 arrived by land alone.

Eventually the gold seekers spread out over a wide area. Historians often divide California's Gold Country into two regions. Different sources describe the exact boundaries of these regions in different ways. I usually think of the Mother Lode area (also known as the Southern Mines) as extending from the town of Mariposa (in present Mariposa County) northward to the community of Placerville (in present El Dorado County). The Northern Mines stretch from Placerville north.

Many people think the Northern Mines are in the most beautiful part of the Gold Country. Today a two-lane road winds through much of the area. Appropriately, this road is known as State Route 49.

The Northern and Southern mines make up California's major gold belt, and it is here that most of the Gold Rush took place. However, it is important to remember that gold has also been found in other parts of the state, including areas in southern California.

The Forty-Niners staked claims throughout much of the Gold Country. When they found "color" (signs of gold) they built camps. Soon tiny mining towns dotted the Sierras. They were nestled in valleys, perched along creeks, and tucked into canyons—anywhere the "pickins" were good.

The mining towns were a blaze of color and excitement as long as the gold lasted. But sooner or later the pay dirt played out, or word of a bigger strike spread throughout the town. Then the miners would often pack up their digging tools and follow their rainbow to the next "pot of gold," leaving behind a trail of empty ghost towns.

What's in a Name?

Many of the places where the argonauts found gold had no names. Or, if they did, the names were unknown to the prospectors (gold seekers) who explored the valleys and canyons of the Sierras. So it was natural for the miners to make up their own place names. Often these names contain memories of life in Gold Rush times.

Sometimes the miners invented names that described the area, like Grass Valley, Prairie City, and Big Oak Flat. Sometimes the names suggested the miners' country or nationality. Names of this type include Dutch Flat, Chinese Camp, Negro Bar, German Canyon, Scotchman's Creek, and Spanish Dry Diggings.

Several of the camps were named for a person, such as the individual who first discovered gold at the site or who had made an impression on the folks who lived there. This category includes such names as Jamestown, Jacksonville, Jenny Lind, Carson Hill, Shaw's Flat, Knight's Ferry, and Goodyear's Bar.

Some names tell right away how or why a camp was named. You can probably guess the reason for names like Poverty Flat (which was near Rich Gulch), Double Springs, Rattlesnake Bar, Flea Valley, and Skunk Gulch.

Other colorful names only hint at the stories behind them. A good example is Sorefinger. How do you suppose this

mining camp got its name? Did a miner drop a huge nugget on his finger? Did a burro take a nip out of an unsuspecting prospector's hand to let him know who was boss (or to remind him it was dinnertime)?

With a little imagination, you can come up with any number of reasons for strange names like Sorefinger. Maybe an argonaut caught a finger in a crevice while he was searching for gold—and exposed a pocket of pay dirt when he freed it! These are only guesses, of course, but I must admit it was fun making up the tales. Perhaps you would enjoy making up stories for place names like Humbug Canyon, Ten-Cent Gulch, Chucklehead Diggings, Shinbone Creek, and Salt Pork Ridge.

Making up colorful stories is fun, but sometimes the true tale is even better than the ones we imagine. Sorefinger is a good example. When I did some serious "digging" (research), I discovered that the true story was even more exciting than my make-believe ones.

According to an aged account, the story stars a giant of a miner who was called "Shorty." Not long after the camp got its start, some of the miners suspected that someone was robbing their sluices (boxes used to separate gravel from gold). The robberies apparently were taking place at night while the miners slept. Naturally, the miners were unhappy about being robbed, and Shorty decided to take matters into his own hands.

Finding a place to hide where he could watch the action, the big fellow settled down to wait. Sure enough, shortly before dawn a shadowy figure crept toward a sluice. Shorty waited until he had the robber dead to rights. Then he took aim and fired his gun at the figure.

As you may have guessed, the bullet struck the thief in the finger. Although he was able to get away, the clumsy bandage wrapped around his wound made him easy to spot. Luckily for him, the camp was not yet fully aroused. The culprit was able to exit the area before a mob could gather and string him up to the nearest tree.

Even though the thief disappeared from the scene, the episode was not soon forgotten. Thanks to Shorty, the robber was given the nickname of Sorefinger—and so was the camp. In this way the story lived on and perhaps served as a warning to newcomers about what happens to those who don't play by the rules!

A Good Town for a Hanging

It was a good thing for Sorefinger that he was able to make a quick exit from the camp that he had been robbing. Otherwise he probably would have ended up with something a lot worse than a sore finger! With no police on hand to keep order, Gold Country miners dealt with thieves and other lawbreakers themselves. Often the penalty for stealing was a quick hanging.

One Gold Country community even gained its name from this rough form of justice. The camp was originally known as Dry Diggings because of a shortage of water at certain times of the year. (Among other things, the miners used the water to wash the gold from the gravel.) Before long, the camp was known by an even more colorful name.

Dry Diggings was one of the first settlements to spring up after the argonauts began drifting away from Coloma. According to some sources, James Marshall (the man who found gold at Sutter's Mill) said that he had a part in helping to found Dry Diggings in the summer of 1848. Other sources credit two (or possibly three) other prospectors with the find. With the help of several Indians, these men reportedly took up to $17,000 in gold from a narrow ravine in a week's time!

When word of this rich strike spread throughout the Sierra foothills, it created quite a stir. From far and near, people rushed for Dry Diggings. Soon it was one of the most sought-out sites in the territory.

As with many of the early mining camps, in the beginning crime was not a concern. But as the community grew, along with the good folks came the bad. Soon robberies and murders were creating anger and fear. As things went from bad to worse, the townspeople decided something had to be done. Ganging up on the bad guys, the enraged residents brought a vigilante style of law and order to the community.

(A *vigilante* is a member of a committee, or group, that captures and punishes criminals without the help of the official government.)

Vigilante justice often meant lynchings (hangings). The first lynching to take place in Dry Diggings made many of the town's hoodlums sit up and take notice. On this occasion, not one but *three* men were strung up at the same time! It seems that the trio of thugs were accused of stealing 50 ounces of gold dust from a Frenchman. The three men were captured and speedily tried. When they were found guilty, the vigilante committee decided that justice could best be served at the end of a rope. At a later date, two Frenchmen and a prospector from Chile were also sent swinging. Their crimes are not even remembered today.

As word spread of "necktie parties" and floggings (whippings), the town of Dry Diggings acquired a new and grisly name. In 1849 the community became known as . . . Hangtown!

In time law and order began to take hold, and the town became one of the most populous of the early mining settlements. Eventually the citizens decided that Hangtown was no longer a suitable name for their community. After some discussion, they narrowed down the choices for a new name to two. One was Ravine City, which the camp was sometimes called in its earliest days. The other choice was Placerville (*placer* is a term for deposits containing gold particles that can be obtained by washing).

As you know if you've ever been there, Placerville won out. Today picturesque Placerville is at the junction of Highways 49 and 50. Instead of lynchings, the town is known for being a popular stopping-off place for people crossing the Sierra Nevadas.

A Deadly Mistake

As I mentioned earlier, a number of Gold Country settlements were named in memory of a particular person. An example is the mining camp called Yankee Jim. But even though we know

who the camp was named for, the *why* isn't so clear. Before me are three respected sources, each one telling a different tale about the man in question.

The first source suggests that Yankee Jim may not even have been a Yankee. Usually this name refers to someone who was born or lived in the United States, especially the northern states. However, this account suggests that Yankee Jim actually hailed from Ireland.

Wherever Yankee Jim was from, he was looked upon as something of a scoundrel. According to this source, though, he had another claim to fame. The source states that Yankee Jim was the first person to find rich gold deposits on the ridges between the North and Middle Forks of the American River. (Before Yankee Jim's discovery, much of the gold that was found in this area was taken from the river bars.)

Like many lucky fortune hunters, Yankee Jim tried to keep his find a secret. As so often happened, he didn't succeed. Word of the find leaked out, and excited argonauts raced to the region.

With the "pickins" being good, more and more miners arrived on the scene. Soon a camp sprang up near Yankee Jim's diggings, and the settlement became known for the man who started the "rich ridge" rush.

So much for the first account. The second source tells quite a different tale. It indicates that Yankee Jim was actually from Australia. In addition, this account highlights Jim's exploits as a horse thief.

Being old and wise in the ways of stealing horses, Yankee Jim was successful at this trade for quite some time. Then one of his victims decided to check the nearby ridges to see whether he could find his animals. His search led him to a corral hidden high on a remote section of a ridge. In the corral were his horses, as well as other animals that had recently been stolen.

When the corral was traced to Yankee Jim, the thief quickly hightailed it out of the territory. It's a good thing he did, too. The men of the Gold Rush had little use for horse thieves. The usual penalty for such a crime was a necktie party at the nearest tree!

The strange thing is that Yankee Jim might have become wealthy beyond his dreams if he had decided to make his living in a more respectable way. According to this account, a wandering prospector came upon the ridge corral not long after the horse thief fled. The prospector decided to try his

luck at the abandoned site. To his surprise and delight, he found the dirt to be rich in gold!

Needless to say, it wasn't long before a town was born. Taking the name of Yankee Jim, the community became one of the most prosperous settlements in the area and one of Placer County's largest mining camps.

These two stories illustrate how legends and lore can grow up around the people and place names of long ago. Unfortunately, I can't tell you how much is fact and how much is fiction in these accounts. And there are still other Yankee Jim tales—including an account I've saved for last because it's my favorite one of all.

According to this story, Yankee Jim was a road agent (a bandit who robbed stagecoaches). So successful was he at this trade that he is compared to such famous Gold Country stage robbers as Joaquin Murrieta and Black Bart. However, unlike those other highwaymen, Yankee Jim operated in a comparatively small area around the camp that bears his name.

The Placer County outlaw's robberies were well planned and expertly carried out. The miners and stagecoach victims had only one clue concerning who he was—his "Yankee" accent!

As the robberies increased, the miners who entrusted their gold to the stage company became more and more upset. They swore that if they ever caught the thief, "they would hang him first and try him afterward!"

Unfortunately, the miners meant what they said. At the height of the robberies, a newcomer walked into a saloon at the edge of the mining camp and ordered a drink. Upon hearing the stranger's Yankee accent, the bartender poured him a tall one and quickly exited through the rear door to spread the word.

Minutes later a band of local miners entered the saloon. Wasting no time, they seized the surprised stranger and strung him up to a nearby tree.

Sadly, the local vigilantes were in too much of a hurry. Much to their dismay, the robberies didn't stop after the lynching of the newcomer. They hadn't caught the outlaw after all! However, about a month later the *real* Yankee Jim was wounded by a stagecoach messenger. This time they were sure they hanged the right man!

As the story ends, the two Yankees were buried side by side, with one extra-wide tombstone marking the spot. Carved on the stone were a pair of hands and a short poem. The first hand pointed to the real Yankee Jim, while the second hand pointed to the innocent victim. By the first hand were the words, "Here lies the body of Yankee Jim." The closing stanza near the second hand read, "We made a mistake, and the joke's on him."

3 BANDITS AND BADMEN

Black Bart, the PO8

The rhyme on Yankee Jim's tombstone (see previous chapter) reminds me of another poem, one that has become a popular part of Gold Country lore. If Yankee Jim really *was* a road agent, he probably would have admired the remarkable success of the poem's author—a fellow stagecoach robber by the name of Black Bart.

Many people think of Black Bart as the King of the Highwaymen. Other Gold Country gangsters before him were better known for such things as murder and mayhem. But for the pure "sport" of stagecoach robbing, Black Bart was in a class by himself.

Black Bart was known for always being polite, always working alone, and always saying "please" when he asked for the "treasure box." (Unlike most Californians familiar with stagecoaches, Black Bart referred to the strongbox that was kept under the driver's seat as a treasure box.) This well-spoken "gentleman bandit" successfully robbed 27 stage-coaches before he was caught!

Even in his appearance, Black Bart was not your run-of-the-mill bandit. Stagecoach drivers learned to keep a sharp eye out for a shotgun-toting highwayman dressed in a long linen duster (a light, coat-like garment worn over clothes to keep the dust off). Besides the duster, Black Bart was set apart by the flour sack he wore over his head (complete with eye holes to see through).

There were other things that made Black Bart different from other road agents. One of them was his habit of making his getaways on foot, carrying his bedroll with him. Another was the double-barreled shotgun he used as a "persuader." Bart was also unusual in refusing to rob the passengers aboard the stages (he preferred the valuables in the "treasure boxes" and mail pouches).

Most unusual of all, the polite bandit became known for leaving poems at his robbery sites. The poems boasted the signature of "Black Bart, the PO8 (po-ate)." One of them goes like this:

> *Here I lay me down to sleep,*
> *To wait the coming morrow,*
> *Perhaps success, perhaps defeat,*
> *And everlasting sorrow.*
> *Let come what will I'll try it on,*
> *My condition can't be worse;*
> *And if there's money in that box*
> *'Tis munny in my purse!*

You might think that the handwritten poems could be traced, but the crafty Black Bart used a different style of writing for each line of verse. As you can imagine, the poems—combined with his unique costume and polite manner—made him the talk of the territory. And as you will see, it wasn't his poems that eventually tripped him up. It was his handkerchief!

Twenty-seven times the poet-outlaw robbed a stage of its valuables and made his getaway. Then came the event that brought about his downfall.

The incident happened during Black Bart's 28th stage robbery. The holdup took place at Funk Hill, near the mining town of Copperopolis. The name of the site is strangely fitting. One meaning of the word *funk* is "a state of extreme depression." What happened after this robbery certainly must have put Black Bart in a funk!

Bart's troubles began when he left a handkerchief at the scene of the crime. To this day, history buffs debate whether the handkerchief had blood on it. Some say that it did, and that the blood came from either a gunshot wound or else a cut the bandit received while opening the strongbox.

Whether the handkerchief was bloody or not, what we know for sure is that it had a laundry mark on it. The mark was traced to a laundry in San Francisco. From there it was a short step to identifying the handkerchief's owner.

That man turned out to be a dignified older gentleman who was well known and well respected in San Francisco society. Known as Charles Bolton, he hobnobbed with the rich and had friends in high places, including the police department! There were also rumors that he had important ties to the mines.

Well, as it turned out, Bolton had ties to the mines, all right! Or maybe I should say that he had ties to the *gold* that came from the mines and disappeared from the strongboxes of stagecoaches. Much to everyone's surprise, it was this dapper gentleman who turned out to be the dreaded stagecoach robber Black Bart!

Yes, as strange as it seems, the most successful road agent of them all was a respected figure in San Francisco society. As Charles Bolton and as Black Bart, he lived a double life. But regardless of which life he was leading, the famous Gold Country bandit was always a gentleman!

Following his trial, Bolton was sentenced to six years at San Quentin Prison to pay for his deeds. Considering the number of holdups he committed, many people thought that six years behind bars was not enough. But after weighing all the evidence, the judge decided differently. After all, the polite Black Bart never hurt anybody, and he never robbed a helpless passenger. Maybe the judge decided that "Black Bart, the PO8" wasn't such a bad guy after all . . . especially since he managed to hold up 27 stagecoaches *with an empty gun!*

"Beware of Bad Associations"

Nobody ever topped Black Bart when it came to holding up stagecoaches, but there were many other outlaws who operated in the Gold Country. One of these badmen was a former doctor who liked to be called by the colorful name "Tom Bell the Highwayman."

Tom Bell's real name was Thomas J. Hodges. Hodges worked as a doctor in his home state of Tennessee, and during the Mexican War (1846–1848), before turning up in the Sierra foothills. There he decided to give up doctoring and try his luck at such things as gold mining and gambling. Unfortunately, his luck wasn't good, and eventually he turned to banditry.

This decision proved to be Hodges' undoing, for bad luck continued to follow him. In 1855 he was arrested and thrown in jail. It may have been this experience that prompted him to take the name of Tom Bell. One account indicates that he "borrowed" the name from a small-time crook who once operated in the Auburn area (in present-day Placer County). By using a false name, the account explains, he hoped to keep his "good name" out of the prison records.

The newly named Tom Bell soon broke out of jail in the company of a fellow convict named Bill Gristy. The pair wasted little time in organizing an outlaw gang. The gang made life miserable for folks in the Northern Mines through such activities as holdups, burglaries, and cattle rustling.

Bell was the brains behind the band of badmen. Often he had the gang break up into small groups and commit crimes in different locations at the same time. At each encounter, the outlaws led their victims to believe that they were being robbed by Tom Bell. As a result, different victims gave different descriptions of "Tom Bell." The conflicting accounts did much to confuse the sheriff and others who pursued the bandits.

To add to the confusion, there were several descriptions of the elusive Mr. Bell's personality. To some of the victims, he was a rough, tough bandit. Others saw him in a totally different light.

According to one tale that has been handed down, the bandit leader wasn't *all* bad. As the story goes, the real Tom Bell was taking part in a robbery. When the unlucky victim tried to escape, Bell's partner, Bill Gristy, shot the man in the leg. Instead of making his getaway, Bell put his doctoring skills to work. The outlaw patched up the wound and flagged down an oncoming wagon. Lifting the victim into the wagon, he told the driver to pick his path carefully so the wounded man wouldn't be jostled too much.

Like Black Bart, Tom Bell eventually pushed his luck too far. His downfall began when he and his associates tried to rob the Marysville/Comptonville stage, which was carrying $100,000 in gold! Unfortunately for the bandits, the holdup was botched when an unsuspecting horseman rode into the ambush area a short time before the stage was due to arrive. Trying to clear the area of any unwanted people, three of Bell's gang set off after the lone rider. To Bell's dismay, the stage

arrived before the trio returned, and he was forced to attempt the robbery with only two of his men.

The robbery erupted into a fierce gunfight. Two passengers were wounded in the shooting, along with the armed stage messenger riding in the "shotgun seat" beside the driver. Worse still, two people were reported killed—one of the bandits, and a woman passenger aboard the stage.

When the dust settled, Bell and the remainder of his gang were nowhere to be seen. But the attempted robbery left the Gold Country in an uproar. One newspaper even called the incident "the boldest robbery ever chronicled." With so much attention being given to catching the bandits, Bell's days were numbered. Less than two months later, he was captured near Knight's Ferry in the Southern Mines.

Once again, frontier justice was swift. After being given a few hours at most to get his things in order, Bell was hanged from a sycamore tree.

Just before he died, Bell wrote two farewell letters. One of them was to his mother. In the letter he blamed himself for the fix he was in. He also offered some advice to his "old and youthful friends." He told them "to beware of bad associations, and never to enter into any gambling saloons, for that has been my ruin."

Bell's last words are an appropriate ending to the story of this doctor-turned-outlaw. And even though his letter was written nearly a century and a half ago, it's not bad advice to follow today.

The Most Dreaded Desperado of Them All

Tales of Gold Country gangsters like Black Bart and Tom Bell could easily fill an entire book. But of the many badmen who roamed the Sierras, one stands out as the most dreaded desperado of them all—Joaquin Murrieta.

To history buffs familiar with the Gold Country, Murrieta is as famous as Jesse James or Billy the Kid. They know him as one of California's most notorious outlaws—a man who struck fear into the hearts of the "gringos" (newcomers to the area, usually Americans). Yet this same man was a hero to many miners of Mexican and Spanish descent who sometimes protected him and helped him escape.

The legend of Joaquin Murrieta has grown so large over the years that it is nearly impossible to separate fact from fiction. Some writers even question whether there ever was such a man! Historians have debated this topic for more than a century. Several of them have come to the conclusion that there *was* a real badman by the name of Joaquin Murrieta, but they say that he and his men have been given the credit (or the blame) for many crimes that weren't their doing at all.

Although we may never be certain about all the details of Murrieta's life, let me share with you one of the accounts we have. To begin with, the future bandit and his wife (as well as other members of the Murrieta party) are thought to have come to the Sierra foothills from northern Mexico. Like other fortune hunters, they were seeking gold, perhaps near the settlement of San Andreas. (The location might have been Saw Mill Flat, or any one of several other Gold Country communities that have become part of the Murrieta legend.) It was there that a group of miners (probably Americans) changed the course of Murrieta's life.

Approaching his camp, the miners attacked Joaquin and his wife, and proceeded to take whatever they pleased. Unable to stop them, the enraged Murrieta vowed to get revenge on each of the cowardly miners who took part in the assault.

So it was that Murrieta started down the outlaw trail. He began by fulfilling his vow to even the score against the men who had intruded upon his camp. But he didn't stop there. Along with a band of followers who rode with him, he and the bloodthirsty bandit Three-Fingered Jack spread terror among miners throughout the Gold Country. The Murrieta gang quickly became notorious for robbing at will, holding up stagecoaches, rustling cattle, and stealing from the rich. The outlaws killed when necessary (and sometimes when it wasn't), terrified whole towns, and ambushed posses that attempted to capture them.

Things eventually got so bad that lawmakers in the California State Legislature got involved. In May, 1853, they authorized Captain Harry S. Love to raise a company of mounted Rangers to capture "the party or gang of robbers commanded by the five Joaquins."

The mention of *five* Joaquins brings us to an interesting point. In the early 1850s the gold fields were full of men who were down on their luck and who chose to lead a life of crime. Some of these men had backgrounds similar to Murrieta's, and at least five of them boasted the first name of Joaquin! Sadly, because Murrieta was the best known of the five, he and his band were blamed for many Gold Country attacks that they were not involved in.

Armed with his special commission from the legislature, Love and his hand-picked Rangers set off in pursuit of the five Joaquins, with Murrieta at the very top of their list. Their quest led them through many wrong turns, to several dead ends, and over hundreds of miles of fruitless searching.

Finally the frustrated Rangers got a tip. A suspicious band of men were camped in a remote canyon (near the Fresno County community of Coalinga). Thinking that they had Murrieta cornered at last, the Rangers eagerly planned an attack.

Soon the canyon echoed with the crackle of gunfire. When the struggle was over, at least two of the gang members lay dead. A quick check of the bodies brought a cheer from the victorious Rangers. One of the dead outlaws was identified as Joaquin Murrieta, and another as Three-Fingered Jack!

But before long the cheers turned to frowns. Almost immediately after the shootout, people began to wonder whether it was *really* Joaquin Murrieta whom the Rangers had killed. Love and his men collected the reward, but some who knew the famed outlaw disagreed. When the head of the supposed gang leader was put on display, they said it *wasn't* the head of Joaquin Murrieta! According to these people, the real Murrieta had fled the Gold Country and returned to Mexico.

To this day, no one knows for sure what really happened to the notorious outlaw. Some history buffs still believe that Joaquin Murrieta spent the rest of his life back home in Sonora, Mexico. If they are right, maybe the most dreaded desperado of them all died peacefully as an old man, his life of crime and vengeance only a memory.

But if so . . . who *did* perish in that fierce shootout with the California Rangers?

Justice—Gold Country Style

When badmen didn't die in shootouts, the miners of the Gold Country had other ways to deal with them. Many of the early Gold Country diggings didn't have judges, sheriffs, police departments, or even jails. For this reason justice was often in the hands of the people who lived and worked in the area. Sometimes the punishment fit the crime, and sometimes it didn't.

Of course, people in those days had their own ideas about what was fair and just punishment. An example is hanging someone for horse stealing. To us, this punishment may seem cruel and unfair, but it was common throughout much of the West. Back then, a man could be ruined by the loss of his horse. Stringing up horse thieves was one way to discourage people from stealing a man's most important possession.

As I mentioned in an earlier chapter, another "popular" form of punishment was flogging, or whipping. Offenders sometimes were flogged with rods as well as whips. Usually the blows were struck on the wrongdoer's back. This type of

public whipping was fairly common in the Gold Country. Often the offender was forced to leave the mining camp after being flogged.

There were other forms of mining justice, too. Depending upon the seriousness of the crime, the culprit sometimes got off with just a "tongue lashing" (scolding) before he was told to hightail it from the territory.

In comparison to being flogged or hanged, this may seem like a "light sentence." To many miners, though, it was not. Being cast out of a camp—and away from one's friends—was looked upon by some as a powerful form of punishment. To them, companionship was extremely important.

Just *how* important is shown by a story that takes place in the tiny town of Colfax (Placer County). It seems that a popular Kentucky miner was found guilty of murder. Instead of being strung up to the nearest tree, he was given a choice. He could leave the town forever—or he could be put to death.

So strong was the bond between the Kentuckian and his friends that the unhappy man chose death over being banished from the area. Preferring guns to rope, the convicted murderer calmly took his place in front of an aged oak tree. With seven rifles pointed at him, he bravely smiled, saluted his friends, and fell to a barrage of bullets!

Other Gold Country punishments included such things as shaving the guilty party's head, branding, and cropping off ears. An especially popular pastime was to fine the offender. At times the money from the fines no doubt found its way to the nearest saloon, where the locals could help celebrate the settlement.

In rare cases, when a miner was found guilty of a crime, he was left alone to decide his own fate. A story about one such incident tells of a prospector who was convicted of murder. The man was told that he could choose his own punishment. As he pondered the problem, the miner proceeded to get drunk. Then, a bit groggy from the liquor, he climbed a tree, put a rope around his neck, and jumped!

Whether or not tales like this are true, they help us to appreciate what life was like for the men who sought their fortunes in California's Gold Country. You can also hear an echo of the rough justice (and humor) of those days in the following poem. The poem was etched on the headstone marking the grave of a horse thief. It makes a fitting conclusion to this chapter on bandits and badmen. Here it is:

Horse Thief

He found a rope and picked it up,
And with it walked away.
It happened that to the other end
A horse was hitched, they say.
They took the rope and tied it up
Unto a hickory limb.
It happened that the other end
Was somehow hitched to him!*

*From *The Strange West*, by Craig MacDonald. Copyright 1986, Pacific Bell (A Pacific Telesis Company).

4 WHAT THE FORTY-NINERS DID FOR FUN

Joke or Justice?

When the Gold Rush was in full swing, more than 300,000 eager fortune hunters swarmed over the Gold Country. Most of them probably came to the gold fields with dreams of "getting rich quick." But only a very few saw their dreams come true. The rest returned home, or drifted off to new places, no richer than when they came.

The sad truth was that life in the mines was hard—much harder than most of the newcomers had imagined. After crossing the plains or braving the voyage by sea, most of them discovered that thousands of fortune hunters had already beaten them to the diggings. Perhaps they had pictured huge nuggets of precious metal just waiting for someone to find. If so, all but a few were soon disappointed. Much of the "surface" gold was pocketed before they arrived. In most cases, it took a lot of back-breaking work to separate even a tiny bit of gold from the dirt and gravel.

Many of the gold seekers in 1849 and 1850 worked from dawn to dusk, six or even seven days a week. For hours at a time they waded in cold, snow-fed streams, or attacked the hard ground with digging tools until their backs ached and their arms felt as heavy as lead. In heat and cold they prospected in steep, rocky canyons and along the rugged ridges of the Sierra foothills. Often all they had to eat was salt pork and beans. Many became exhausted, injured, or sick.

All in all, the miners' lives were hard and dreary. But like people everywhere, they found ways to take their minds off their troubles. A favorite way was to play tricks and practical jokes. If life was hard, at least they could laugh about it!

The practical jokes took many forms. Sometimes one miner played a trick on another, and sometimes whole settlements got into the act.

According to one story, an especially clever trick even allowed a man to escape being hanged for murder! Several versions of this tale have been passed down through the years, and it may have grown in the telling. Still, there are old-timers today who swear it is true, and it continues to be a favorite "nugget" of Gold Country lore.

One version of the story goes something like this. In November of 1853, a miner by the name of Peter Nicholas ventured into the town of Columbia (Tuolumne County). While he was there, he got into a scuffle with a miner named John Parrot. During the skirmish Parrot was stabbed. He slumped to the ground, seriously wounded.

With Parrot apparently dead or dying, Nicholas was seized and thrown into jail. Soon, however, an angry mob gathered and broke into the jail. Shouting and cursing, they marched Nicholas to the hanging tree.

The mob nearly had the noose around the helpless man's neck when word came that Parrot was still alive. Reluctantly, the angry miners gave up the idea of hanging Nicholas and returned him to the jail.

The wounded Parrot lingered on for a short while, and then he died. This time, Nicholas was given a proper trial. Once more it seemed his own life was about to end, for he was found guilty and sentenced to death.

But the lucky Nicholas cheated the hangman again, thanks to a trick played by some of his friends. It seems that his pals had managed to get hold of a petition that was circulating around Columbia. The petition was a message to

the state legislature demanding that the state capital be moved to Columbia. It had already been signed by 10,000 people.

The petition gave Nicholas's friends an idea. Carefully, they clipped off the wording about the state capital. In its place, they wrote a message requesting a pardon for the condemned man. Hastily they sent the phony petition to the governor, signatures and all!

So impressed was the governor with the 10,000 signatures that he promptly signed the request! With the pardon in hand, Nicholas's friends wasted no time getting him released. And, as the story ends, by the time the trick was discovered, Nicholas was long gone!

Many a miner has enjoyed a hearty chuckle over this story. Was it a joke, or justice? You be the judge!

Jokes That Backfired

As you might expect, many of the miners' practical jokes revolved around gold. One popular joke was to send a "greenhorn" (newcomer) off in search of gold in some unlikely place. After a great deal of time and trouble, the greenhorn would return, blushing and empty-handed.

This trick may have been one of the miners' favorites, but more than once it backfired. One example takes us to Hangtown. When two recent arrivals asked about a good place to dig, a grizzled miner pointed to a spot at the base of a nearby hill. A handful of the miner's friends were in on the joke. All of them agreed that the ground was barren. The trick was to make the greenhorns *believe* they had struck it rich.

The newcomers dug and dug. When they lugged a container of dirt to the stream in hopes of washing the gold from it, the miner's pals gallantly offered to help. As they were showing the greenhorns how to separate the gold from the dirt, one of them slipped a good-sized nugget into the pan.

When the nugget was found, the miners shouted with glee and ran to the site to stake a claim. Laughing at the show his friends had put on, the grizzled miner stood his ground. Lazily, he continued to work the greenhorns' pile of dirt. To his surprise, he turned up several chunks of gold! Suddenly he realized that the soil was actually rich with the yellow stuff. Flabbergasted at the find, he, too, raced to the base of the hill—only to discover that all of the available land had been claimed!

As it turned out, the "phony" site proved to be extremely profitable. Before long the victims of the miner's prank were being hailed as the owners of one of the richest mines in the area!

A similar joke took place near Mokelumne Hill (Calaveras County). One day a black prospector arrived on the scene and asked some of the more experienced miners to point him toward a likely spot to dig. Glancing about, they nodded toward a hill that had already been gone over by a number of gold seekers. Thanking the miners, the grateful greenhorn gathered his things and headed for the hill.

Several days passed, and the newcomer was neither seen nor heard from. Many times the "locals" must have nudged one another and enjoyed a good laugh at his expense. But a week after being directed toward the hill, he was back at the camp—showing off all the gold he had found! Needless to say, the jokesters were soon rushing for the "barren" hill!

A few miles away, near the community of Jackson (Amador County), the familiar story was repeated. The supporting cast in this Gold Country drama were—as usual—the veteran miners. The stars of the tale were three young argonauts from Germany.

In this account the greenhorns were directed toward a scattering of mine tailings. (Tailings were what was left after a mine had been worked. They were also referred to as waste, remains, leavings, and leftovers.) Busily setting to work, the eager diggers dug *through* the tailings and struck a rich vein of gold in the ground underneath!

As the old saying goes, "He who laughs last, laughs best." Perhaps only a few of the Gold Country's practical jokes backfired, but it's fun to think of the "victims" having the last laugh. If you're like me, you enjoy stories in which the losers turn out to be winners.

One final tale of this kind takes us to a place called Rich Bar (Plumas County). A group of American miners were arguing with a band of Frenchmen over which party had reached the bar first. With the rights to work the bar at stake, the furious miners were ready to settle the argument once and for all—with guns!

Fortunately, before any shots were fired, cooler heads prevailed. Instead of an all-out war, it was decided that each company would choose a representative to fight it out with

49

fists. The winner's group would stay put, while the loser's party would leave.

Each group picked its strongest and most agile member to represent it. Soon the fight was on. With the men from each company loudly cheering their heroes on, the two mountain men put on an amazing show. Blood flowed freely as the weary warriors clobbered each other without mercy, but neither would give in. Finally, the punch-drunk Frenchman was no longer able to stand. The Americans shouted in triumph as their man was declared the winner. The bar was theirs!

After reviving their fallen fighter, the disappointed Frenchmen kept their promise and packed up their digging tools. Heading up the bar, they staked their claim at another site.

As you've probably guessed, it was the Frenchmen who had the last laugh. Much to the dismay of the Americans, their new diggings proved to be richer than the ones they had left! So, even though the Frenchmen lost the Battle of Rich Bar, they certainly won the war!

The Best Jokes of All

California's Gold Country stretches more than 200 miles up and down the western slope of the Sierras. So it seems strange that two of the region's "best jokes" took place just a stone's throw away from each other, in Calaveras County. One was a memorable prank, while the other was a humorous story that became famous around the world.

The site of the practical joke was Bald Hill, an area near the community of Altaville. In 1866 an argonaut from neighboring Angels Camp reported an amazing discovery. He said that he had found an aged human skull at the bottom of a mine shaft—more than 125 feet below the ground! The mysterious skull became big news throughout the Gold Country. In time, it became famous around the world.

What made the skull so interesting? Well, it appeared that it had been taken from a geologic formation (layer of earth) that was extremely ancient. In fact, the formation dated back to a time *before* people were even supposed to be in California!

The "impossible" discovery baffled scientists. The bony find became known as the Pliocene Skull, after the name of a prehistoric period. But Pliocene times were far too early for human remains. If the skull was genuine, it would force scientists to change their ideas about how and when people first came to North America.

For many years scientists wrangled over the age of the skull and whether it was truly prehistoric. Finally, the skull was inspected by a group of leading anthropologists (scientists who study old bones and other prehistoric remains). They concluded that the skull *was* indeed very old. But they also agreed that it *didn't* date back to "pre-human" times.

As it turned out, the scientists could have saved themselves a lot of trouble. Apparently, the skull was nothing more than a clever practical joke! Later it was said that some of the locals around Angels Camp knew all along that someone had "planted" the skull at the bottom of the mine shaft (perhaps a worker or the mine's owner). There were even

rumors that the head belonged to a long-dead Indian, and that it had been stolen from the office of a local doctor!

Even though most agree that the Pliocene Skull was a hoax, it helped to make Calaveras County famous for more than its millions of dollars' worth of gold. Meanwhile, a joke of another kind was also adding to the county's fame.

This story also begins in the mid-1860s (shortly before the Pliocene Skull began making news). At that time Angels Camp was host to a man by the name of Samuel Clemens. One winter night, Clemens and some of his friends were warming themselves in the bar of the Angels Hotel. While they were there, they heard a local fellow (perhaps the bartender) tell a funny tale about a frog.

The story went something like this. Sometime around 1849 or 1850, a resident of Calaveras County had himself a pet frog. Now, this wasn't just any ordinary frog. Its owner had spent countless hours training it to jump farther than any other frog. The frog even did somersaults and jumped high in the air to catch flies!

Being mighty proud of his pet, the man sometimes carried it with him in a small box. One day a stranger visited the camp and became curious about what was in the box. The frog's owner promptly displayed his pet and bragged that it was a champion jumper. Why, he would even bet anyone that his frog could outjump any other frog in Calaveras County!

The stranger was impressed with the man's enthusiasm, but he could see nothing special about the frog. If only he had a frog of his own, he said, he might be willing to bet.

The local man assured the newcomer that he would gladly fetch him a suitable jumper. When the stranger nodded his approval, the man left his pet with him and went to a nearby swamp to find a worthy opponent.

While the frog's owner was gone, the newcomer began having second thoughts about the bet. He didn't want to back out, but he didn't want to lose his money, either! Then he had an idea.

Making sure no one was looking, he picked up the frog, opened its mouth, and poured in some bird shot (tiny balls of lead used as ammunition). With the frog weighted down by the heavy metal, he put it back on the ground and waited for its owner to return.

Soon the frog's owner was back with a second frog, and the contest was ready to begin. Each man gave his jumper a pep talk and a pat on the head for good luck. With a gentle nudge to get the frogs hopping, they settled back and hoped for the best.

Well, you can imagine what happened. The stranger's frog happily jumped away, while the local man's pet squatted meekly on the ground, looking fat and foolish.

Stunned by his defeat, the disheartened owner paid the newcomer. After watching him saunter off, he turned to his prized frog (which still hadn't moved an inch). For the first time he realized how full his pet looked. Stooping to pick it up, he gasped at how much the frog weighed! With a frown, he turned his pet upside down to see what was going on.

Just then the weighed-down beast gave a noisy belch. Out of its mouth came a bellyful of bird shot!

Oh, but the man was furious! Putting his pet down, he raced off to find the newcomer. But the trickster knew better than to hang around. Unfortunately for the owner of the "champion jumping frog of Calaveras County," the stranger was nowhere to be found.

The prank recounted in this tale is a good one, but the *real* story isn't about the frog. Instead, it's about the man who chuckled over the story on that long-ago night in the Angels Hotel. If it hadn't been for Samuel Clemens, very few people today would know the tale that became famous as "The Celebrated Jumping Frog of Calaveras County."

You see, it was Clemens who rewrote the account and went on to become one of America's best-loved writers. By the way, the name he signed to that story over a century ago was "Mark Twain." And it was as Mark Twain that he became the world-famous author of such books as *The Adventures of Tom Sawyer* and *Adventures of Huckleberry Finn*.

Together with the hoax of the Pliocene Skull, Twain's "tall tale" helped to put Calaveras County (and Angels Camp) on the map. In fact, since the late 1920s Angels Camp has staged an annual frog jumping contest. The event is known around the world, and contestants as well as spectators come from far and near to join in the festivities. It's hard to know which is most famous—Calaveras County's gold, its "fake" prehistoric skull, or its fictional frog!

Entertainment, Gold Country Style

Besides jokes, pranks, and tall tales, the Forty-Niners also amused themselves with other kinds of entertainment.

Unfortunately for some, they often spent their money on gambling and drink. When a strike was made and miners stampeded to the new diggings, saloonkeepers and gamblers were quick to follow in their footsteps. As a result, many of the mining camps boasted more than their share of "drinking holes" and gambling halls.

Columbia, the "Gem of the Southern Mines," is a good example. According to reports that describe Columbia in the 1850s, scattered about the bustling town were 2 theaters (including a Chinese theater that boasted 40 actors), 4 banks, 8 hotels, and 27 general stores. But even the general stores were outnumbered by the town's 30 saloons, not to mention its 143 gambling palaces!

In the early days of the camps, the establishments that offered liquor and games of chance were among the miners' favorite gathering places. It was here that they could drown their sorrows or celebrate their good fortunes, mingle with other fortune seekers, and renew friendships. They traded the latest gossip and learned about new strikes. And, of course, they spent the gold they had worked so hard to get.

Gold and gambling seemed to be a common thread that linked many of the miners' lives together. In the gambling houses, card games were the favorite pastime. Among the most popular were monte, seven-up, faro, and poker. Even when the miners were far from an established camp or town, they often gathered to play a few hands of cards. It was a rare argonaut who didn't carry at least one deck of cards in his pack.

Besides cards, miners invented all kinds of contests and wagers. Combining competitions with chances to win a bit of gold, they bet each other on whatever struck their fancy. Contests were arranged to determine the swiftest runner, the longest jumper, the straightest shooter, the fastest swimmer, the strongest wrestler, the best horseshoe pitcher, or the most talented flapjack maker.

Whenever there was a contest, there were people willing to risk some hard-won gold on the outcome. On one occasion, two miners even made a bet on which one could hold his breath the longest. Unfortunately, the winner was unable to celebrate his victory, because the effort of the contest caused his heart to burst!

Dances were another popular pastime. In the early days there seldom were enough women to provide dance partners, but that didn't stop the argonauts. Some of them would tie a rag around one arm or use some other form of identification to indicate they were willing to take the woman's part, at least for a few dances.

Music for the dances was usually provided by the miners themselves. Often someone in the crowd had a fiddle or a harmonica, and sometimes other musical instruments that the argonauts had brought to the gold fields would appear.

When enough instruments could be found, informal "concerts" were held on Sunday afternoons. Often a concert was preceded by a parade through the town or camp. Music also accompanied religious festivals, which often had their own parades.

Other popular Sunday-afternoon attractions included sporting events involving animals. As with the contests between humans, the miners used these events as occasions for making bets. A good deal of gold changed hands at cockfights (rooster fights), horse races, bullfights (pitting man against bull), and bull-and-bear fights.

Probably the most brutal of the animal "sports" was the bull-and-bear fight. These events actually dated back to the days of the Spanish missions, but Gold Rush gringos took to the fights with gusto. Venturing into the mountains, the miners would capture a large and ferocious grizzly bear to bring back to the camp. Meanwhile, a large and equally ferocious bull would be obtained from a valley ranch or from one of California's fabled early ranchos.

When it was time for the fight, the bear was placed in the center of a heavily barricaded arena and secured with a chain. Then the bull was led into the arena. Usually the bull was left unchained, but sometimes the animals were chained together by a hind leg. (This practice was more common during mission days.)

If things went as planned, the two beasts were soon locked in a savage battle to the death, with hundreds of spectators cheering them on. Sadly, fans of this brutal sport weren't satisfied unless they saw considerable blood and gore.

I'm glad to report that the Forty-Niners also enjoyed more pleasant forms of entertainment. Many of them eagerly looked forward to visits from touring theatrical groups, lecturers, and other performers. Once in a while a small circus would travel around the territory, featuring such attractions as horse shows, dog acts, and jugglers.

Good or bad, performances of all kinds were sure to attract a crowd. And if the argonauts liked what they saw, they often showed their appreciation in the best way they knew how—by showering the stage with coins, nuggets, and small buckskin pouches of gold!

5 WOMEN OF THE GOLD RUSH

Little Lotta Crabtree

In the early days of the Gold Rush, there were very few women in the Sierra foothills. The married men who joined the rush for gold usually left their families behind, as the rough-and-tumble mining camps were no place to enjoy a family life. One source estimates that early in 1849 there were only 2 women for every 100 men in the gold fields!

By 1850, more women were coming to the camps. Even then, men still outnumbered women by more than 10 to 1. So, when a woman happened to visit or settle in one of the outlying camps, it was a special event.

Many of the first women to visit the gold fields and mining towns were entertainers. Singing, dancing, and putting on skits, they were usually given a warm reception by the hard-working and homesick miners.

Perhaps the performer who was given the warmest reception of all was Lotta Crabtree. When she first came to the attention of the miners in the mid-1850s, Lotta was a bright-eyed and spunky young lady of about seven years of age. Before long, the little red-headed lass was the Gold Country's biggest child star.

According to several accounts, Lotta's first public performance was at a blacksmith shop in the colorfully named camp of Rough and Ready (Nevada County). Reports say that she danced an Irish jig on the top of an anvil (a heavy block of iron or steel that blacksmiths hammered on to shape metal). Some accounts describe the blacksmith tapping out the beat with his hammer, while others suggest that Lotta danced to the rhythm of clapping hands.

Either way, the lively performance was a hit. The gold seekers who witnessed it applauded heartily and hailed young Lotta as an up-and-coming "Fairy Star" (a singing and dancing child of exceptional talent).

The dance atop the anvil may have started Lotta's career as an entertainer, but her first venture onto a real Gold Rush stage took place a bit later, when she was eight or nine. The place was a camp called Rabbit Creek, which is now known as La Porte (Plumas County).

It's uncertain whether Lotta danced in a saloon or in a small theater, but sources do agree that her "vigorous Irish jig" was a smash success. The miners—especially those of Irish descent—loved the happy-go-lucky lass and her costume of green. Whistling and cheering, they threw nuggets and pokes (pouches) of gold dust at her feet to show their appreciation. Rumor has it that one miner tossed a gold coin worth 50 dollars (a *lot* of money back then) onto the stage!

Excitedly Lotta gathered up the gold and delighted the crowd by stuffing it into her shoes! With that, a tradition was born, as showers of gold from the audience became a regular feature of Lotta's performances.

After that memorable first night, Lotta's star began to shine. She soon added more dances and other acts to her routine. She sang tender ballads, played the banjo, and acted out skits and pantomimes.

Before long, miners in towns and camps up and down the Sierras were clamoring for "little Lotta," and she began touring the settlements with her mother. Traveling with them were two men who helped promote the show and set up the stage. On occasion the men also played guitars, fiddles, or

drums to help entertain the crowd and provide music for Lotta's routines. Some sources say that one of the men was also Lotta's dance and singing teacher.

As Lotta traveled from place to place, her legend grew. The miners flocked to her performances and took her to their hearts. No doubt she and other Fairy Stars reminded homesick gold seekers of the families they had left behind. But no other young performer became as famous as Lotta.

Lotta performed in saloons, dance halls, dinner houses, theaters, and tents. Everywhere she went, after the show coins and gold were tossed her way. Sometimes the cheering miners even carried her about the room on their shoulders!

Lotta spent several years touring the Sierras. Along the way, she became quite a skilled actress. In later years, she was even known to play as many as six parts in one play! Eventually, though, the Gold Country began to change. As many of the miners pulled up stakes and moved on, Lotta and her mother decided to move to San Francisco.

It was in the "City by the Bay" that Lotta began thrilling audiences of more sophisticated city folk. From San Francisco she went on to tour other cities and states. In one place after another, she was wildly received by adoring fans. The former "Fairy Star" of the gold fields even gained international fame by performing in far-off England!

In her mid-40s Lotta decided that it was time for her to retire. Bidding her disappointed fans goodbye, she stepped down from the stage.

Lotta never married, and after her retirement she continued to live with her mother. Because her mother had managed her well, they were quite wealthy. As the years went by, the two of them enjoyed many happy times in their 17-room house in northern New Jersey.

In 1905 Lotta's mother died. Lotta followed in 1924, at the ripe old age of 77. When she died, her fortune was worth millions of dollars. She left all her money to charity.

Little Lotta Crabtree never forgot her California beginnings. In 1875 she hired a Philadelphia company to make a statue for the people of San Francisco. It was Lotta's way of thanking them for the love they had shown for her. It was also her way of expressing her own love of the city.

A few years later, Lotta visited San Francisco for the dedication of the statue. Today "Lottie's Fountain" (or "the watering spot," as old-timers called it) can still be seen. The statue—a cast-iron monument about 30 feet tall—stands at the intersection of Geary, Market, and Kearny Streets in beautiful San Francisco.

Other Gold Country Women to Remember

Lotta Crabtree isn't the only Gold Country woman whose story is remembered today. Another well-known star of the gold fields is often credited with helping Lotta learn how to "sing and dance and toss her curls." Lola Montez was her name, and she was a glamorous figure in Gold Rush days.

Lola was a favorite topic of conversation among the miners. Among her claims to fame were her unusual dances, especially her famous Spider Dance. People also gossiped about her lavish lifestyle. She liked to throw fancy parties, drink the finest liquors, and eat expensive imported food. She also kept an odd assortment of pets, including monkeys and grizzly bears. Perhaps most shocking to people in the 1850s, this strong-minded woman enjoyed smoking Spanish cigars!

Other female entertainers were also popular with the Forty-Niners. One was Caroline Chapman, who was described as a "comedy queen." Lola Montez briefly appeared with her on the San Francisco stage. Another was Sue Robinson. Like Lotta Crabtree, she was a Fairy Star of the Gold Rush era.

If the miners welcomed touring entertainers, they were even more excited when a woman actually decided to settle in the Gold Country. Rumors tell how the residents of a town in the Southern Mines gave a huge welcome to one lady when she moved to their community. The locals decorated the main street in her honor, formed a mile-long procession to greet her, and serenaded her with a brass band!

As time went on, more gold seekers and other new-comers brought their families with them to California, and more wives began joining the men who were already at the diggings. A number of the Gold Country womenfolk recorded their experiences in letters and diaries. Their writings have given us some of our best descriptions of life in the mines.

Among the best-known of these documents are the letters of Louise Amelia Knapp Smith Clappe. Known to her friends and most history buffs as Dame Shirley, Louise was married to a young doctor by the name of Fayette Clappe. The couple arrived in California in 1849 and spent some time in San Francisco before moving on to the Feather River area of the Northern Mines.

From the Feather River, "Dame Shirley" wrote a number of letters that have been preserved in a book called *The Shirley Letters*. Many of them were written to her sister in Massachusetts. Of course, in those days (early 1850s), people couldn't just call up their friends and relatives on the telephone, so they put their news and thoughts in letters.

Dame Shirley's letters described her surroundings in detail. She also told about activities associated with the mines, including mining techniques. And she shared her observations of the miners' personalities, right down to their drinking habits!

Another well-known batch of letters are those from Mary Ballou to her son. Mary's letters were written from a camp along the American River. Parts of the letters are in the form of a journal (a record of daily events and thoughts). They almost let us peek inside her and relive her heartaches and frustrations.

Like many other women who shared the adventure of life in the mines, Mary worked at a boarding house. Gold Country wives often took on this type of work, doing such things as cooking in a boarding house, delivering food to the miners, or taking in laundry. Interestingly, many of them found that they could make more money than their husbands who were constantly chasing the golden dream!

One such woman was Luzana Stanley Wilson. With her husband and children, Luzana arrived in Nevada City (Nevada County) in 1849. Looking around the settlement, she realized that there was a need for an eating house and a place for miners to stay. Not wasting any time, she began cooking meals for the miners. Soon a hotel was built (the El Dorado), and Luzana and her husband were kept busy running the establishment.

Before long the Wilsons had more money than they knew what to do with. Then Luzana began loaning money to the miners (she charged them 10 percent interest per month). As their profits rolled in, the Wilsons stuffed their extra cash under the floorboards of their bedroom. Thanks to Luzana's efforts, they were on their way to becoming very rich. At one time, they had over $200,000 stashed under their floor!

Then disaster struck. A blazing fire raced through Nevada City. The hotel—and all the Wilsons' money—went up in smoke. Like many of the other merchants, the Wilsons were forced to start over again.

The names (and nicknames) of many other Gold Country women are still remembered by those with an interest in California's colorful mining days. Here I'll mention just a few you might want to learn more about.

One woman known only as Juanita has an unhappy claim to fame. She was the first woman to be hanged in California!

Then there was the colorfully named Madame Moustache. She operated an elegant gambling hall where no swear words or bad behavior were allowed.

Speaking of colorful names, One-Eyed Charley Parkhurst was a skilled and courageous stagecoach driver who disguised herself as a man. No one knew Charley was a "she" until after she died!

Although she wasn't in disguise, a woman known as Madame Pantaloons shocked the argonauts by working her mine in men's clothing. Another female mine owner was Hetty Green, whose Old Eureka Mine helped her become one of the world's richest women.

Besides the few I have mentioned, there were thousands of women who played a part in the rich history of the western slope of the Sierras. Above all, it was the women who helped to turn the rugged camps and towns into respectable communities, complete with churches, schools, and libraries. So let me end this chapter with a tip of the hat to all the adventurous and hard-working women of California's Gold Rush!

6 LUCKY STRIKES AND LOST OUTLAW LOOT

Gold Was Found in the Strangest Ways

With tens of thousands of argonauts combing the Sierra foothills, you might wonder how some of them found any gold. Certainly, as more and more people came to the gold fields, the precious metal became harder and harder to find. However, with new tools and methods of mining, even many of the late arrivals were able to gather a vast amount of the yellow stuff.

As I mentioned in an earlier chapter, finding gold usually involved a lot of hard work. But a surprising number of lucky miners struck it rich by accident! If old stories can be believed, gold was sometimes found in very strange ways.

Many accounts of accidental finds have been passed down through the years. A typical tale comes from the same general area where the Gold Rush began. According to the story, three Frenchmen uprooted the stump of a tree on the Coloma road and found $50,000 in gold!

A second account also takes place near the American River's South Fork. It seems that a popular miner had died and was about to be buried. One of the other miners happened to be a preacher, and he was called upon to say the proper words.

In the midst of the prayer, the preacher heard excited whispers from the mourners who were kneeling by the grave. Looking up, he saw what the excitement was all about. One of the miners had been sifting some of the freshly dug dirt through his fingers—and had found gold!

Instantly the funeral was put on hold as the preacher and the mourners took the body from the grave and began digging. Fortunately for the dead man, the ceremony was finished later at a site where the soil was less rich.

Speaking of preachers, a minister named Davidson is said to have discovered a profitable mine in Amador City (Amador County). The reverend wasn't burying anyone at the time. Instead, he was digging a foundation for his church!

As you might expect, there are quite a few tales that involve some kind of digging. One such story involves a gold seeker from Germany who was digging a hole for his tent pole when he found a three-ounce nugget!

And before moving on, I would like to touch on a second account involving graves. According to this tale, a fellow by the name of Oliver Martin was digging a grave for his dead partner when he turned up a nugget worth $22,270!

In Grass Valley (Nevada County), George McKnight had his cow to thank for his good fortune. It seems that McKnight was chasing the runaway animal when he stubbed his toe on a rock. Instead of hopping in pain, McKnight was soon jumping for joy. The rock turned out to be laced with gold!

Another miner made his lucky find after staking his mule to a peg in the ground. When he pulled out the peg, he found the hole sprinkled with gold!

Then there's the tale of the hunter who shot a grizzly bear. The bear fell over a cliff and landed on a ledge below. Making his way down the cliff, the rifleman discovered that the ledge was flecked with yellow! Before long, miners from miles around were making a beeline to the gold-bearing cliff.

Another animal-related find features a gopher instead of a bear. Apparently, a miner named Jenkins noticed that the water to his rocker had stopped flowing. (A rocker is a cradle-like contraption the miners used for washing gold.) Upon investigating the problem, Jenkins found that a gopher hole was draining his source. He probably was a bit annoyed—until he discovered that the gopher's hole was richer than his! In sharing the hole with his furry friend, he averaged more than $1,000 a day for the next month.

A storekeeper with the odd name of Bennager Rasberry also boasted of an accidental find. While on an outing near Angels Camp, he got a ramrod stuck in his gun. Unable to remove the rod, he decided to *shoot* it out.

Pointing the gun at a manzanita bush on a nearby hill, Rasberry blasted away, and out flew the ramrod. The only problem was that the rod now was stuck in the manzanita bush!

Muttering to himself, Rasberry walked over to the shrub and yanked it out of the ground, roots and all. As you may have guessed, when he looked in the hole, he found gold! Reportedly, the lucky storekeeper took nearly $10,000 from the area in less than three days.

Another account involving a shooting features a pair of gunmen who were said to have been members of the Joaquin Murrieta gang. The gangsters were holed up near the community of Volcano (Amador County) when they got into an argument over a woman. In the shootout that followed, a stray bullet struck a rock—and exposed a vein of gold!

Upon seeing the gleam of gold, the warring bandits quickly called a truce. And, the story goes, the former badmen turned into quite wealthy miners.

While on the subject of badmen, I should mention a thief by the name of Daniels. Upon being captured, Daniels was sentenced to hard labor in the Hangtown rockpile. However, while breaking rock on his first day of work, he found enough gold to buy his freedom!

Sometimes a lucky find was a "dream come true"—in more ways than one. One such story tells of two men from a southern state (one was a slave, and the other was his owner). Each of the men dreamed that there was gold under a certain cabin in the camp. Deciding to trust their strange dreams, they bought the cabin and dug up its floor. Underneath they found gold valued at nearly $20,000!

On rare occasions, finding gold was as easy as falling off a log—or tumbling into a gulch. At a place called Steep Gulch, a one-time sailor named Clark had too much to drink one night and slipped into the gulch on the way back to his cabin. After dislodging some rocks in his attempt to climb out of the gulch, he slid to the canyon's bottom amid the stones. At that point the groggy Clark decided that he might as well spend the night where he lay and try again in the morning.

When he woke up the next day, Clark looked around and found particles of gold in the rocks he had dislodged the night before. You can bet he wasted no time in staking a claim. In less than three weeks, he was richer by some $70,000!

Perhaps the best story about a sudden change of fortune involves a grizzled miner who dejectedly sat on a rock, complaining about his lack of luck in finding gold. Upon listening to his woes, a passerby suggested that he look under the rock he was sitting on. With a shrug, the aged argonaut took the stranger's advice. Sure enough, he found gold!

In thinking about that happy ending, I must admit that the passerby had some wise advice. Instead of sitting around and complaining about a problem, it's a good idea to "get off your rock" and do something about it!

The Sad Saga of Rattlesnake Dick

Most of the fortune seekers who came to California during the Gold Rush were honest and hard-working. To these argonauts, "treasure" meant handfuls of nuggets, pans filled with glitter, and rocks streaked with yellow. Unfortunately, there were also those who left honesty behind as they chased their dreams of riches. According to some old-timers, these men are responsible for another kind of treasure that is scattered about California to this day.

One such bad guy is known as Rattlesnake Dick. His real name was Richard H. Barter. The son of a British army officer, Barter came to the Sierras from Canada. He acquired his nickname after settling in a camp called Rattlesnake Bar (Placer County).

There are various accounts of Barter's early days in the Gold Country. According to some of them, he worked hard and tried to keep out of trouble. But bad luck seemed to follow him, and twice he was arrested for stealing. On the first occasion a jury found him not guilty. The second time he was arrested (for stealing a mule), it turned out that someone else had taken the animal. Still, Barter felt that he had been tagged as a thief, and he decided to move to another camp.

Making his way to the community of Shasta (Shasta County), Barter took the name of Dick Woods and tried to make a new start. Unfortunately, other argonauts from the Rattlesnake Bar area also chose to try their luck in the diggings around Shasta. When they recognized Barter, they spread stories about his past. Soon the word was out that he wasn't to be trusted.

If this information is accurate, you can understand why Barter might have become bitter. Perhaps it was experiences like these that led him to take up a life of crime. If he was going to be treated like a bad man, maybe he figured he might as well be one!

What we do know is that it wasn't long before Barter (or "Woods") traded his gold pan for a gun . . . and the saga of Rattlesnake Dick began.

At first Rattlesnake Dick busied himself with small-time crimes like robbing sluices, holding up travelers, stealing cattle, and making off with stray mounts. (A sluice, or sluice box, was one of the devices used to separate gravel from gold.) But when he met up with others of his kind, his life began to change. Before long he was involved in bigger crimes involving numerous outlaws.

One of these crimes was a robbery that has been described as one of the biggest in the Gold Rush. Rattlesnake Dick was the mastermind behind the plot to hold up a mule train that was transporting a sizable load of gold from the Yreka area in Siskiyou County to the town of Shasta. It is said that the gold was worth between $80,000 and $100,000!

Dick laid his plans carefully, and at first it seemed that they were going to pay off. The gang boldly robbed the mule train and made off with the goods, mules and all! But then a snag developed in Dick's getaway scheme.

The plan called for Dick to meet the other bandits at a prearranged spot with fresh, unmarked mules. Unfortunately for the gang, Dick was caught stealing mules near his old haunts in Placer County. So, while his partners in crime waited for him with the loot, Rattlesnake Dick was cooling his heels in the Auburn jail.

The other members of the gang hid out for a time and managed to evade a posse that was seeking the hijackers of the mule train. When Dick still didn't show up, they knew they had a problem. The gold was too heavy for them to carry, and they had turned the original mules loose because they bore the brand of the shipping company. Needing to get away before

their whereabouts were discovered, they decided to bury part of the loot and take the rest with them.

Most sources agree that the gang buried about half of the gold and transported the other half to Placer County. Upon nearing Auburn, the outlaws met up with the posse that was looking for them. In the shootout that followed, the leader of the gang was killed. His companions were captured along with the gold.

But what about the gold that had been buried? Interestingly, it was the gang leader who had personally stashed it away. When he was killed in the gunfight, the secret of the bonanza's location died with him.

No one has ever found the secret cache of gold. To this day Rattlesnake Dick's loot is said to lie somewhere beneath the ground, one of the many outlaw treasures just waiting for a lucky "prospector" to find!

As for Dick himself, his story has a tragic ending. Because he was already in jail when the robbery and shootout occurred, he was released after serving out his term for mule stealing. He soon resumed his life of crime, and he saw the inside of many jails before he was done. But he also perfected a talent for breaking out of them!

Eventually, however, Dick's luck ran out. The end came about three years after the mule train robbery. One night in

1859, Dick and a companion were leaving Auburn when he was recognized by three local citizens, including two lawmen. The trio formed a mini-posse and set off in pursuit.

The men caught up with Dick and his partner about a mile out of town and demanded their surrender. When the outlaws refused, the night was filled with the sound of gunshots. One of the possemen was killed and another had his hand shattered. But some of the posse's bullets also found their mark—two of them in Dick's body!

The wounded outlaw managed to get away, but he was badly hurt. The next morning his lifeless body was found about a mile from the site. Besides the two bullets in his body, there was also one in his head! Next to his body (or, some say, clutched in his hand) was a note. There are different accounts of what the note said. The one I like best states that scribbled on the paper were these words: "Rattlesnake Dick dies but never surrenders, as all true Britons do."

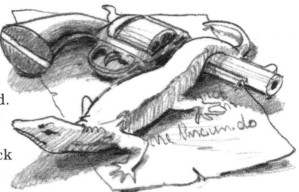

So ends the tale of another Gold Country gangster. But you can be sure that Rattlesnake Dick's story will live on in the minds of those who dream of hidden wealth . . . and lost caches of outlaw loot.

More Tales of Lost Outlaw Loot

Rattlesnake Dick is only one of the Gold Country badmen whose names are linked with lost treasure. Among the others are two famous outlaws discussed in an earlier chapter—Tom Bell and Joaquin Murrieta.

One story involving Bell says that he stashed a sizable hoard of money and jewels somewhere just east of the town of Stockton (San Joaquin County's gateway to the Southern Mines). No one knows for sure how much the cache is worth, or exactly where it was hidden. (One source suggests that it may have been buried in a cave.) Stories still circulate about this lost treasure, and fortune hunters continue to search for it to this day.

There are a number of treasure tales associated with Joaquin Murrieta. Even though most of the accounts about his activities take place in the Gold Country, there are also many stories about his lost loot in other parts of California. In fact, a tale or two about his hidden wealth has sprung up almost everywhere Murrieta spent time or had a hideout.

Sometimes the fabled bandit didn't even have to be in the area for a story to get started. One such tale involves a freight wagon filled with gold that Murrieta and his gang are said to have stolen from the Northern Mines. Some of his most trusted men were chosen to transport the valuable cargo to the bandit chieftain's home in Sonora, Mexico. Before they could complete their journey, the wagon was attacked by Indians near the Carrizo Wash in southern California. After killing the guards and driver, the Indians helped themselves to the gold, burned the wagon, and hid the rest of the cargo in a burial cave. What became of Murrieta's gold? Your guess is as good as mine!

Another Murrieta tale takes us to the town of Bagby in Mariposa County. (The original town site is now covered by the backwater of the Exchequer Dam.) It was near Bagby that Murrieta supposedly found a cave filled with skeletons. The

cave seemed like a perfect place to hide his cache of $60,000 in gold, because he figured that the skeletons would scare superstitious people away. Perhaps he was right, too, since the treasure he stashed in the cave is still waiting to be found.

Incidentally, that story reminds me of another tale involving a treasure cave. Even though this account doesn't involve outlaw loot, it fits in well here because this second cave is also said to be located near Bagby.

As the story goes, in the 1850s a Mexican miner stored several burro loads of gold in a cave in the Bagby area. As his treasure hoard continued to grow, he decided he needed help with his mine. Not wanting to share his secret with anyone outside his family, he concealed both the mine entrance and the entrance to his cave. Then he set out for Mexico to get some of his relatives to help with the work.

Unfortunately, the miner never returned to claim his treasure. While he was in Mexico, he got into a fight and was killed. Neither his mine nor the cave has ever been found.

Getting back to Murrieta, another account involving one of his lost treasures takes us to the Merced River, near the town of Snelling (Merced County). It was on the banks of the river that the Murrieta gang made camp after robbing and killing some Chinese miners along the Mokelumne and Calaveras Rivers. While in the area, Murrieta hid a small iron chest that contained $30,000 in gold.

The chest remained hidden until sometime in the 1930s. At that time the chest—or one resembling it—was picked up by a gold dredger (a barge or boat with a dredge mounted on it). Unfortunately, before anyone could get to the chest, it slipped from the dredge and fell into a deep hole where divers were unable to find it.

A second story about a badman's treasure chest also takes place in the Snelling area. In the mid-1850s a lone highwayman is said to have robbed a stagecoach and buried its strongbox near Snelling. Afterward the gunman made his way into town, where he visited one of the saloons. While he was there, a fight broke out. In the brawl that followed, the badman was severely wounded.

The outlaw knew that he didn't have long to live. Haltingly he told the story of the robbery and the hidden strongbox. Unfortunately for those who had gathered around, the location of the chest remained vague, and the strongbox was never found.

Some present-day treasure seekers think that the strongbox may have been covered by a dredger that worked the area. Others wonder whether it was this chest—and not Murrieta's—that slipped off the dredge in the 1930s. If so, the whereabouts of Murrieta's buried treasure remain a mystery.

A final account about Mr. Murrieta and his lost loot takes us to the Calaveras Forest near the town of Murphys (Calaveras County). It was in this vast wooded area that the famed bandit leader and his gang are said to have stashed a sizable amount of gold. No one knows for sure how much gold they hid, but sources agree that it was worth considerably more than $100,000!

These stories are only some of the countless tales of outlaws who left loot in and around California's Gold Country. If even a few of the accounts are true, there is enough bandit booty around to keep modern-day fortune hunters busy for years to come! While I could continue with such stories, it's time to move on to the next chapter so I can tell you about some treasures that are *not* associated with bad guys.

7 TALES OF TREASURE

Buried Treasures

As we learned in the last chapter, the Gold Country's hidden wealth includes more than the vast amount of yellow metal that Mother Nature sprinkled about the gold fields. According to numerous tales, there are also many kinds of treasures that were placed there by human hands.

It wasn't just outlaws who had reason to conceal their gold and other valuables. Without convenient banks nearby (at least as we know them today), many of the miners also chose to hide their wealth. They used all kinds of hiding places, including caves, hollows of trees, and under the floorboards of cabins. But probably most of them buried their treasures in the ground.

If old stories can be believed, many of those treasures are still there today. Like other areas in the West, the Gold Country is rich in tales of buried bonanzas and lost wealth waiting to be found. And even if the miners' wooden chests and buckskin pouches rotted away long ago, many of the valuables they contained (such as gold, coins, and jewelry) should still be in good shape.

One well-known tale of a lost treasure takes us to Drytown in Amador County. According to the story, a fellow by the name of Joe Williams worked a profitable mine in a nearby area called Murderer's Gulch. Upon cashing in his gold for money, he had a carpenter build several small wooden boxes. After filling each box with gold coins, he buried them. Supposedly they were never buried alone, as there was always at least one box within four feet of another.

Later, when Williams was close to death, those who knew about his boxes begged him to tell them where the money was hidden. However, the stubborn miner only growled, "Nobody will find it in a hundred years!"

Well, 100 years have come and gone, and apparently the treasure is still buried. So if you ever get to Drytown and you feel lucky, you might want to do a little prospecting of your own. The treasure hunt would be worth it, since Williams' cache is said to contain $80,000 in gold coins!

A similar tale takes place near the little town of Lotus (El Dorado County). Strangely enough, this account also involves $80,000 in lost gold coins!

As the story goes, a miner successfully worked several rich pockets in the Lotus area and then had his findings converted into coins. The miner didn't want to risk having the coins transported to San Francisco for deposit in a bank. Instead he told a trusted friend that he was going to bury his bonanza for safekeeping.

A short time later the miner became ill and died. His belongings and property were thoroughly searched, but the stash of coins was never found.

A third story takes us to a Nevada County camp called Bloody Run. The camp's rather grisly name fits this tale, for the episode involves a miner who was killed for his gold.

Back when the diggings around Bloody Run were profitable, a man named Mayberry took about $40,000 in gold from his claim. Burying the yellow metal near his cabin, Mayberry continued working his mine. Some time later, robbers paid him a call and demanded his gold. In the struggle that followed, Mayberry was killed.

As the story ends, the robbers never found the gold the miner had stashed away. Like the other treasures discussed in this chapter, Mayberry's riches are thought to remain in the bank of Mother Nature.

Bean Pots, Fruit Jars, and Iron Kettles

Some of my favorite stories about Gold Country treasures involve the unusual containers that the miners sometimes used to hide their wealth in. These containers came in all shapes and sizes. In fact, gold seekers were likely to make a "treasure box" out of just about anything they had handy, as long as it could hold a collection of nuggets or coins.

A good example is a bean pot that was buried near Coulterville (Mariposa County). In Gold Rush days, Coulterville was a boom town boasting several thousand people. It was during this time that a Frenchman built a wood-burning smelter on the banks of nearby Maxwell's Creek. (A smelter uses heat to separate gold from chunks of ore.)

A second Frenchman, who was employed by the first, worked a nearby placer claim on his time off. After gathering a quantity of gold, he put it in a bean pot and buried the pot near the smelter. From time to time he unearthed the pot and added more gold to his stash. Before long, he figured, he would have enough to pack his belongings and return to his homeland.

Unfortunately, before he could realize his dream, the homesick Frenchman was killed by a falling beam at the smelter. According to legend, the nugget-filled bean pot is still buried near the creek.

Over the years a surprising number of people have used jars and bottles to hold their hidden valuables. One cache of this type is said to be in the Placerville area, near Highway 49. What makes this treasure special is that it was buried on two different occasions, by two different men—and both times it brought death to the man who buried it!

Although the account of this cursed treasure is a bit sketchy, here is what I learned. Long ago (nobody seems to know exactly when), a man secretly buried a half-gallon-sized fruit jar on a farm near Placerville. The jar was filled with 50-dollar gold pieces. Not long after, its owner was murdered—probably by someone who was seeking the treasure.

Several years later, the man who now owned the farm found the container, still filled with coins. This man buried the jar again at another spot. Amazingly, a short time later he, too, was killed by people who were searching for the money! As the story ends, the fruit jar and its contents remain unclaimed somewhere on the Placerville area farm.

Another account involves a treasure contained in bottles. This tale takes us to a place called Hawkins' Bar, which was near the headwaters of the Tuolumne River (Stanislaus County). The bar was named for Old Man Hawkins, who had both a claim and a cabin in the area.

According to the stories that have been handed down, Hawkins hid the gold he took from his claim in pickle bottles, and then buried the bottles around his cabin. When Hawkins died, his fellow argonauts were too busy with their own claims to bother looking for his stash. Supposedly the gold-filled bottles are still waiting to be dug up by some lucky finder.

Besides jars and bottles, a number of accounts tell of Gold Country treasures buried in iron pots. One of them is similar to the fruit jar tale I shared a moment ago. Like that earlier story, this one also involves a treasure that proved to be a deadly curse to two different men.

According to the story, a rancher who lived near Columbia was known to keep his wealth in an iron kettle. When the rancher disappeared, his friends and acquaintances became concerned. However, the mystery didn't last long, as his body was soon found shoved into some underbrush. With the discovery of the body, word spread that the killer had been after the rancher's wealth.

A short time later a local man was caught and accused of being the murderer. Although he swore he was innocent, the unlucky man was hanged for the crime.

To this day there are many who believe that the hanging was a mistake and that the accused man really was innocent, just as he claimed. As for the iron kettle, it may still be hidden on the murdered rancher's land.

Additional accounts tell of treasures that were stashed in other kinds of containers, including safes, saddlebags, 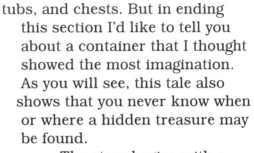 tubs, and chests. But in ending this section I'd like to tell you about a container that I thought showed the most imagination. As you will see, this tale also shows that you never know when or where a hidden treasure may be found.

The story begins with a placer miner by the name of Jacob Henry. Henry worked many streams throughout the Southern Mines, with his last location being in the Columbia area.

One day Henry walked into Columbia's Pioneer Saloon and asked whether he could leave his light wagon in the lot next door while he made a trek to the back country. The saloon's owner liked Henry and appreciated the way he always paid for his drinks in gold, sometimes buying a round for the whole house. He gladly granted the miner's request.

Several weeks went by, and there was no sign of Henry. Most people supposed that he had probably died somewhere in the back country.

Finally a man showed up to dispose of the missing miner's property. No one knew where Henry's team of horses were, so the man was happy to sell all that was left, including a harness and the wagon that Henry had left in the lot. He and the buyer agreed on a price of $5, and the deal was done.

As it turned out, the new owner got quite a bargain. Upon hauling the wagon home, he left it in his yard. After a time, when he was working around his house, he ran short of wood. Remembering that the wagon had an almost-new bed (bottom) in it, he decided to use some of the wood.

As he pried out the wood, the lucky wagon owner made a surprising discovery. The new bed actually covered the old one, and sandwiched in between was Jacob Henry's secret stash—a hoard of 20-dollar gold pieces!

Too Many Treasures to Talk About

Outlaw loot, buried bonanzas, gold hidden in all kinds of containers . . . Truly there are more treasure tales connected with the Gold Rush than I can begin to tell you about. In this section I'll squeeze in a few more stories that have caught my imagination. I hope they will encourage you to do some research and dig up your own nuggets of Gold Country lore.

The first account that comes to mind revolves around a man by the name of Joseph F. A. Marr. In 1851 Marr was the treasurer of Mariposa County. Although different sources tell the story differently, most of them agree that Marr and his horse were killed as they tried to cross a swollen stream (appropriately named Deadman's Creek). Supposedly, Marr was making his rounds collecting taxes when the accident occurred.

Even though Marr's body was discovered the next day, the tax money he had collected was never found. But the lost money is only part of the story.

Apparently, before leaving his house to collect the taxes, Marr had buried another treasure—a hoard of 50-dollar gold slugs worth approximately $15,000!

Now, $15,000 is nothing to sneeze at, but Marr's buried treasure is worth much more than that. Present-day collectors may be willing to pay as much as $10,000 for *each* slug. That makes this missing treasure one of the richest in the Gold Country!

A second account of hidden wealth takes us to neighboring Tuolumne County. It was in the hills near the community of Columbia that a Portuguese miner struck it rich. The miner did his best to keep the location of his mine a secret. He entered and exited the town from different directions, and he waited until after dark to return to his claim so that it would be difficult for anyone to follow.

Even though the miner kept to himself, he was known to those he did business with. Perhaps it was these people who expressed concern about him when he was not seen or heard from for a number of weeks.

As it turned out, they had reason to worry. Some time later the miner was found—dead. However, any thoughts of foul play were soon put to rest. An inspection of the body showed that the miner had died of natural causes.

Not knowing the dead man's next of kin, the local men searched his pockets for clues. It was then that they

discovered part of a letter that was written in Portuguese. Unable to read it, the finders took it to a Portuguese sheepherder to be translated.

The contents of the letter created a mystery that persists to this day. The message indicated that the miner knew he was sick and was going to die. It also said that he had buried $100,000 in his mine, and then sealed the entrance! The miner intended to leave both the money and the mine to the person he was writing to in Portugal. But the letter did not include either the location of his strike or the address of the person it was written to.

As you can imagine, the dead man's letter sparked an eager search for the sealed mine. However, the entrance was never located. To date, the mine, and its treasure, are said to remain unclaimed.

Camp Seco, in northern Calaveras County, is the scene of the next tale. The story takes place in the 1860s, a time when the area around Camp Seco was booming. With plenty of gold to be found, eager fortune hunters swarmed over the claims that dotted the gulches and gullies leading to the Mokelumne River.

Along one such ravine lived a miner from a southern state whom I will call Robinson. When Robinson came to California, he brought his personal slave with him.

I should mention that a number of miners from the South brought slaves to California during the Gold Rush. Some of the slaves braved punishment or death in attempts to escape. Others worked hard to buy their freedom with their labor or with the gold they found. Still others, like Robinson's slave, worked alongside their "masters" and were treated more like partners than like slaves. Happily, slavery was soon to become a thing of the past in the United States, and many of these African Americans went on to become prominent figures in their communities.

Robinson and his slave worked together and found a substantial amount of gold. Then Robinson became sick. Knowing that he was about to die, he told his partner that he had put much of the gold in cans, and buried the cans around the cabin. When the end came, he added, everything he owned (including the cabin, the claim, and the gold) would be his!

Years later, when the former slave was on *his* deathbed, he told the story of the buried cans. Unfortunately, in all the years he lived at the cabin, he never found the gold his partner had buried.

Another treasure tale about a former slave also takes place in Calaveras County. The location of this hidden hoard is Camp San Antone (along San Antone Creek, near the popular mining town of Murphys). The man who stashed the valuables was known as Buster. He was an escaped slave who had made his way to California before the Gold Rush.

When gold was discovered in the San Antone area, Buster found himself in the right place at the right time. The former slave staked a claim and became rich. Reportedly, he hid up to $50,000 in gold and coins near his cabin or in the hills behind it!

When Buster died in 1863, those who knew about his wealth tore down his cabin and searched the ground around it. Legend states that the fortune was never found and that it is still stashed somewhere around Camp San Antone.

Next on my list is a tale that takes place in Alabama Flat (El Dorado County). This once-active mining camp was located near Hangtown (Placerville). Among the argonauts who lived there was a miner by the name of John Chapman. Like some other miners, he liked to boast about the fortune he had buried near his cabin.

One morning Chapman was having breakfast at one of the local eating establishments when he was killed by an unknown assailant. Out of respect for their dead friend, the residents of Alabama Flat waited until Chapman was buried before searching for his hidden wealth. Then they promptly headed for his cabin with shovels in hand! However, even though they dug countless holes in the area around his shelter, they never found the treasure.

More than 100 years have passed since Chapman was killed, but old-timers still talk about his boasts and wonder about his lost fortune. You can understand why they would be interested, since the value of the stash was estimated to be as high as $40,000!

A Lake of Gold

As I hinted in the last section, there are more stories of Gold Country treasures than will fit in this book. Since I have to stop somewhere, I would like to bring this chapter to a close with one last tale. As it should be, this account is about gold—lots of gold . . . in fact, a lake of gold!

As often happens with long-ago events, it is difficult to be certain about all the details of this story. Among other things, sources disagree about who actually discovered the lake—or whether the lake itself is anything more than a legend. With this in mind, I'll draw on several accounts and tell the tale that makes the most sense to me.

The story begins with a man named Stoddard (there is some dispute about his first name). Stoddard is said to have been one of the several thousand argonauts who traveled across the plains in 1849 on their way to the California gold fields. While crossing the rugged Sierra Nevadas on the last leg of his trip, Stoddard and a companion left the party they were traveling with to hunt for food. Unfortunately, they lost their way in the mountain wilderness and became separated from the rest of the group.

For several days Stoddard and his friend wandered around in search of help. During their travels they stumbled upon a picturesque lake nestled in the high country. Upon dropping to their knees to drink from the clear water, they realized that there were hundreds of nuggets lining the lake's shore!

Awed by the sight, the weary wanderers filled their pockets with gold. After resting a while, they resumed their search for their companions, or for some sign of a camp or other settlement.

As they struggled down the west side of the Sierras, they were suddenly attacked by a party of Indians. In the fight that followed, Stoddard was wounded in the leg and became separated from his partner.

Even though the wound slowed him down, Stoddard somehow managed to escape. It may be that the Indians were busy pursuing his partner, for Stoddard's companion was never seen again.

All alone Stoddard continued his painful trek down the mountain. Eventually he reached the outlying camp of Downieville (Sierra County). It was here that he told his story and showed off his gold.

Stoddard's account of the golden lake made him an instant celebrity in the remote outpost. Together with some of the camp leaders, he began making plans to organize an expedition and return to his lake of riches. However, fall had already set in, and the men knew that the high country would soon be blanketed with snow. Reluctantly the eager gold seekers decided to postpone their expedition until the following spring, when the fabulous lake would be free of snow and ice.

As it turned out, the months of waiting allowed Stoddard's story to spread throughout the Northern Mines. The tale grew with each retelling and fired the imaginations of the argonauts who heard it.

By the following May, when the expedition was scheduled to leave, miners from throughout the northern diggings were more than ready to join in. To the dismay of Stoddard and his

new friends, the latecomers lined the streets of Downieville. To a man, they were determined to follow the expedition and claim their share of the lake's wealth!

The organizers of the expedition were unhappy about all the freeloaders who were planning to tag along without paying for the privilege. Still, they knew that waiting longer would only give even more fortune hunters time to arrive on the scene. Deciding to make the best of the situation, they struck out for the high country.

Even in springtime the going was rough. As the argonauts forded icy rivers and climbed steep gorges, the Sierra wilderness began to take its toll on the hangers-on. Many of them returned to Downieville and their home camps. But those who had paid to join the expedition continued to follow the trail Stoddard blazed.

At first the men kept their spirits up by dreaming of untold riches and the shimmering lake of gold. But as the days turned to weeks and the terrain became even more rugged, their mood began to change. Stoddard led them over forested mountain ridges and through rock-filled canyons more than 1,000 feet deep. Still the lake was nowhere in sight. Soon some of the men were grumbling that Stoddard must be crazy. Others wondered out loud whether there really was a nugget-lined lake.

Finally, with the supplies almost gone, the leaders of the expedition told Stoddard that they had had enough. Angrily they gave him 24 hours to find the lake—or be strung up to the nearest tree!

Needless to say, Stoddard was in a fix. Probably he had become hopelessly lost in his effort to retrace his steps and find the lake. With the threat of death hanging over him, he decided to take matters into his own hands.

That night, Stoddard waited until his guards became distracted (or perhaps nodded off to sleep). Then he quietly slipped out of camp and disappeared into the darkness.

Like his former partner, Stoddard was never seen again—at least in California's Gold Country. As for the expedition, it never did find his golden lake.

To this day there are those who discuss the various versions of this story and wonder how much truth can be attached to them. Although there are many unanswered questions, the tale continues to inspire modern-day fortune hunters. Some of them still roam the high country above and beyond the Downieville area hoping to glimpse a picturesque lake tucked away in a secluded glen . . . with handfuls of yellow nuggets lining its shore.

It's only fitting to end this book with the story of the legendary lake of gold. After all, it was stories like this one that changed California history by bringing thousands of Forty-Niners to the gold fields. Often their dreams didn't "pan out," but the stories continued to be told. And even today, there are many who seek out the Gold Country because of the tales they have heard . . . tales of lucky strikes and lost outlaw loot, of buried treasures and golden lakes.

You can be sure that the stories will live on, too. For even though the Gold Rush belongs to days gone by, there will always be new argonauts who are ready to follow in the Forty-Niners' footsteps . . . dreaming California's golden dream.

AUTHOR'S NOTES

Each book in the **History & Happenings of California Series** includes an Author's Notes section. Teachers and students alike use these notes to delve more deeply into "the story behind the story" and to learn more about the **people, places,** and **events** mentioned in the text.

In this connection, I should mention that conflicting sources often make it difficult to know exactly what occurred in days gone by. Of course, this question of separating fact and fiction comes up even when sources agree, or when an event is documented in only one source. Historians must constantly weigh all the evidence they can gather. Did the persons who recorded an incident tell the true story of what took place? Or did they bend the facts for the benefit of their audience, perhaps adding a splash of color to make the tale more exciting? When accounts differ, which one is more credible?

It's important for students to realize that questions like these are unavoidable in history. On the other hand, they are part of what makes history (and historical research) fun. In addition, the legends and lore connected with events like the Gold Rush are very much a part of history. As I mentioned in Chapter 7, it was the *stories* of untold riches that lured thousands of fortune hunters to the gold fields, and so helped to change the history of the Golden State.

With these thoughts in mind, let me begin these Notes with a comment concerning the **Placerita Canyon** site where gold was discovered in 1842. This find, which I describe in Chapter 1, has been called the first discovery of gold "in commercial amounts" in California.

But exactly how much gold is that? Unfortunately, an exact figure is impossible to obtain. Estimates of the amount of gold taken from the Placerita Canyon area range from lows of less than $10,000 to highs of nearly $100,000. Information in the respected book *California Historical Landmarks* (published by the Office of Historic Preservation, California Department of Parks and Recreation) indicates that an estimated $80,000 worth of gold was taken from the region. Based on this figure, I can comfortably say that this 1842 strike was, indeed, a significant find!

Incidentally, if you care to visit the site of the discovery, a Historical Landmark has been placed in the area. It can be found in the Placerita Canyon State and County Park, Placerita Canyon Road, Los Angeles County.

As I indicated in Chapter 1, another lesser-known source of pre-Marshall gold is the **Santa Lucia Mountains.** (You may recall **David Douglas** and his sighting of gold in the roots of a great tree, as well as the mention of mission period treasures and Lost Padre mines.) This coastal range witnessed a "mini" gold rush of its own. Not only did the area produce a surprising amount of gold, but it, too, boasts an abundance of colorful tales. Some of these stories are recounted in the chapters on Missions San Antonio and Carmel in my book *Tales and Treasures of California's Missions.*

Probably the most famous site associated with the start of the Gold Rush is the complex known as **Sutter's Fort.** Today Sutter's Fort is surrounded by the city of Sacramento. It has been restored by the State of California to look as it did during Sutter's time. Sutter's Fort is open to the public and is one of Sacramento's most popular attractions.

Speaking of the beginnings of the Gold Rush, in describing **Sam Brannan's** role in sparking the rush for gold, I briefly touch on the **San Francisco/Yerba Buena** connection. As you may know, the first village to be built where part of downtown San Francisco now stands (near the foot of Telegraph Hill) was originally known as El Paraje de Yerba Buena (the Little Valley of the Good Herb). Through usage the name was shortened to Yerba Buena. The "good herb" in question is described as a white-flowered wild mint that grew in the region. While there are those who may differ, 1847 is generally accepted as the year Yerba Buena officially became San Francisco. Today the name Yerba Buena graces the city's handsome new cultural center, located in the South of Market area.

The first section in Chapter 2 discusses various routes the gold seekers took to California. The most popular water route for those who boarded ships on the East Coast of the United States (primarily the New England area) was around **Cape Horn.** However, even though the term "around the Horn" is generally used to describe the voyage, many of the vessels that went this way did not actually sail all the way around the tip of South America. Instead, they took a narrow channel known as the Strait of Magellan. About 350 miles long, this passageway was considered the most dangerous part of the trip. The strait was named, of course, for Ferdinand Magellan, the Portuguese navigator who is credited with having commanded the first expedition to sail around the world (even though he was killed before the voyage was completed).

Of the combination land/sea routes to California chosen by U.S. residents, the **Panama connection** was the most popular. The majority of the argonauts who took this route were from the middle and southern states. A number of fortune hunters, though, sailed instead to the countries of Nicaragua and Mexico. After disembarking from their vessels, they made their way overland to the Pacific and caught a second ship for their journey up the coast to San Francisco.

In dividing California's **Gold Country** into two regions (as I do in Chapter 2), I must admit my boundaries are flexible. For example, gold *has* been found south of Mariposa (which, for reference purposes, I list as the southernmost point of the Southern Mines). As to the dividing line between the Northern and Southern Mines, some sources prefer the Auburn area (Placer County) to Placerville (El Dorado County). To confuse matters even more, occasionally a source will divide California's Gold Country into three sections—Northern, Central, and Southern.

Chapter 2 also discusses some of the place names that dot the gold fields. Perhaps no other area in the United States boasts such an abundance of colorful names. In fact, over the years some of the gold mining communities (such as **Ravine City/Dry Diggings/Hangtown/Placerville**) were known by several names. Interestingly, some sources state that Dry Diggings was actually called *Old* Dry Diggings. As for the change to Hangtown, sources describe the incident that inspired this name in different ways. You might want to do your own "digging" into this interesting episode.

The tale of **Yankee Jim's** tombstone that ends Chapter 2 is drawn from the book *What's in a Name?* by M. Goethe. While the story may only be folklore, its rough humor is certainly an authentic reflection of Gold Rush days.

Even more intriguing than the colorful place names discussed in the chapter are the fascinating people associated with the Gold Rush. Certainly one of my favorite Gold Country characters is **Black Bart** (Chapter 3). You may wish to check into the life of this famed "King of the Highwaymen" and explore the many tales about his outlaw career. By the way, in case you're wondering how Bart managed to break open stagecoach strongboxes when his gun was empty (prohibiting him from blasting the locks off), he is reported to have carried an axe in his bedroll for just this purpose.

Chapter 3 also tells about the bandit **Tom Bell** and how his attempted robbery of the Marysville/Comptonville stage created an uproar in the Gold Country that eventually led to his arrest. Several sources indicate that the death of the woman passenger had much to do with the public outcry and the ensuing effort to bring to justice the man who master-minded the holdup.

The supposed death of the famous bandit chieftain **Joaquin Murrieta,** as discussed in the same chapter, sparked a controversy that continues to this day. I must admit that I side with those who believe it was *not* Murrieta's head that was exhibited after the shootout with the California Rangers.

My reason for this belief dates back to 1980, when I was privileged to read the reminiscences of a pioneer Monterey

County resident (born along the Big Sur coast in the 1850s). This account, which was written at the request of his family, stated that in 1877—while working as a ranch hand on a Carmel Valley ranch—he witnessed a conversation between a stranger and the ranch foreman. As a young man, the foreman had waited on Murrieta and his gang when they frequented his father's roadhouse in the Sierras. During the talk the foreman mentioned his father's inn, and then asked the visitor if he was Joaquin Murrieta. Acknowledging that he was, the stranger went on to say that he had come back to the area to retrieve some treasure that he and his men had buried many years before! While there is more to this story than I can elaborate on here, accounts such as these make me wonder who—other than Murrieta's sidekick **Three-Fingered Jack**—the California Rangers killed in the Fresno County shootout of 1853.

Incidentally, one respected historian spent more than half a century researching the Murrieta story. He concluded that the head that was passed off as the bandit's, was, instead, the head of a Monterey-area Indian who had served as a hostler for the Murrieta gang.

As discussed at the end of Chapter 3, **justice** for the Gold Country's badmen took many forms. One additional story helps to round out the picture. According to this account, two Placer County men were accused of stealing a bag of sugar, a bag of beans, and three hams. When one jury couldn't reach a verdict, another was called. The second jury found the pair guilty, and the culprits were sentenced to 75 lashes with a whip and banishment from the camp! As I explained in the text, banishment was considered a severe form of punishment. Besides having to leave their friends, the guilty parties were faced with giving up their claim and starting anew in an area where their crime was unknown.

Chapter 4's mention of the famous Gold Country town of **Columbia** brings to mind a story about its aged schoolhouse. The building opened its doors in 1860 and continued to serve as a school until the late 1930s. However, time took its toll on the two-story structure, and as its 100th anniversary approached it was in sad need of repair. Coming to its rescue were teachers and students from throughout California who raised $52,000 (of the $60,000 needed) to restore the facility. Today the aged brick building—complete with bell tower, desks, a pump organ, and stove—helps to remind us of Columbia's proud past. It is also an example of what people can do when they work together. By the way, Columbia today is a State Historic Park and a "must" for those who enjoy learning about the Gold Country and taking a peek into the past.

If you liked the story about the Frenchman and the American who staged a mighty fist fight for the right to remain at their **Rich Bar** diggings, you may be interested to know that the location the losers chose as their "consolation prize" became known as French Gulch. However, like Rich Bar, there is more than one French Gulch in the Gold Country, so do your homework well before you decide to visit the site.

Chapter 4 also highlights **Calaveras County,** the scene of **Mark Twain's** famous "Jumping Frog" story. Among the county's other claims to fame is Carson Hill, which has been described as the richest camp in the Mother Lode. Not only did the Carson Hill diggings produce a staggering amount of gold, but one of the largest nuggets ever found in the United States was discovered there (at the Morgan Mine) in 1854. It weighed nearly 200 pounds and was worth more than $43,000 at the time it was found! With a little research and a calculator, you might enjoy figuring out what this king-sized nugget would be worth at today's prices.

As related in the chapter, another event that helped to put Calaveras County on the map was the famous incident of the so-called **Pliocene Skull.** I think you will agree that Calaveras County was an appropriate location for the find, as *calaveras* is the Spanish word for skulls! The name comes from an event that occurred more than half a century before the Pliocene Skull became known. It was then that Lt. Gabriel Moraga of the Royal Spanish Army came upon a river he called El Rio de las Calaveras (River of Skulls). He so named it because of the many human skulls that were found in the water—the remains of an Indian battle that had taken place there many years before. It was from this river that the name of the county was derived.

If you enjoyed the story of the Pliocene Skull, you might want to seek out a poem by Bret Harte called "To the Pliocene Skull." Harte, like Samuel Clemens (Mark Twain), spent time in the Gold Country when the mountains and valleys still echoed to the sounds of the prospector's pick. He wrote several delightful stories of his own about the area, including such favorites as "The Outcasts of Poker Flat" and "The Luck of Roaring Camp."

In the final section of Chapter 4, I mention that there were 143 **gambling "palaces"** in Columbia in the 1850s. In this context the word "palaces" shouldn't be taken too literally. Although the Gold Country's gaming parlors and gambling houses came in a variety of shapes and sizes, often (particularly in a camp's early days) they were little more than tents. I should also add that even though the Gold Rush is frequently portrayed as a time of rather wild goings on, many miners were content to spend their free time in activities other than drinking and gambling. They read (when books were available), wrote in their diaries, or composed letters to their families back home. Instead of gambling away all their gold, they saved every ounce they could to bring their families to California, or to return home with enough money to buy a farm or start a business. In addition, one of the pastimes that miners throughout the foothills looked forward to was a quiet game of chess!

In Chapter 5 I tell the story of **Lotta Crabtree** and describe how she visited San Francisco for the dedication of "Lottie's Fountain" (usually reported as 1879). While the dedication drew a huge crowd, perhaps the best-remembered event to take place at the base of the statue occurred in 1910. At midnight on Christmas Eve of that long-ago year, the famous opera singer Luisa Tetrazzini sang to thousands of people who had gathered to hear her. When her beautiful voice filled the night air, a hush fell over the assembled crowd, and the people of San Francisco were treated to one of the city's most memorable moments. To commemorate the event, a bas-relief portrait of the opera star was added to Lottie's Fountain.

If you're interested in learning more about Lotta's "coach," **Lola Montez,** you may wish to know that her real name was Maria Dolores Eliza Rosanna Gilbert (Eliza Gilbert for short). While Lola was certainly colorful, women like **Louise Clappe (Dame Shirley)** left a more important legacy from a historian's point of view. As I indicated in the text, Dame Shirley's collected letters provide a wealth of information on what life was like in the mines in the early 1850s.

In telling the story of the enterprising **Luzana Stanley Wilson,** I described the fire that swept through Nevada City and burned the Wilsons' hotel (along with their savings). Fire was a constant worry in the gold fields. In many cases, towns were burned to the ground more than once. However, if the diggings were still profitable, the miners would simply rebuild the town and start over again. Often brick buildings with steel shutters on the windows and doors were used the second or third time around.

In addition to the several notable **women of the Gold Rush** discussed at the end of Chapter 5, I'd like to mention two others you might want to learn more about. One is Jesse Benton Fremont, a gifted writer who was married to one of California's first U.S. Senators. The other is Mary Murphy Covillaud, a survivor of the famous Donner Pass tragedy. The town of Marysville (Yuba County), which became a trade center for the Northern Mines, is named after her.

In Chapter 6 I tell how gold was found in the strangest ways. It's important to add that **"lucky strikes"** were only a small part of the story. As time went on, the argonauts became more and more skilled in finding gold. Instead of trusting to luck, they learned more about the peculiarities of the elusive yellow metal and where it was apt to be found. They also began checking such things as piles of dirt uncovered by rodents and particles of rock that had been crushed by the wheels of passing wagons. Especially in the later stages of the Gold Rush, many a profitable mine or pocket of rich ore was discovered by gold seekers who used their heads along with their hands.

Interestingly, even the late arrivals didn't get *all* of the gold. To this day, gigantic nuggets are still being found. One impressive example from the Mother Lode community of Jamestown (Tuolumne County) was reported in the *Monterey Peninsula Herald* of January 1, 1993, under the headline "California Mine Firm Mum on Its 60-Pound Gold Slab." According to another newspaper item, in 1989—140 years after the Forty-Niners came west—Tuolumne County produced more gold than it did during the entire Gold Rush!

One gold seeker who used his head—but for the wrong thing—was **Rattlesnake Dick.** Curiously, the mastermind behind one of the biggest heists in Gold Rush history wanted to be known (according to one source) as the "Pirate of the Placers." His ambition was never realized, however, as books about bandits almost always refer to him as Rattlesnake Dick.

Rattlesnake Dick's preferred nickname reminds me of another Gold Country badman who is described as having once been a *real* pirate. His name was Jim Scott, and he is one of a number of undesirable characters you will run across if you look into the lives of some of the bad guys who plied their trade in the diggings.

Another bandit you may find worth investigating conducted most of his activities in the Northern Mines, primarily in the Grass Valley and Colfax areas (Nevada and Placer Counties). His name was Louis Dreibelbis, and I think you will be surprised to learn why his mail-order bride sent the sheriff after him.

If you decide to go hunting for one of the **buried treasures** mentioned in Chapter 7, be sure to carry both old and new maps with you. The names of many locations have changed through the years, in some cases several times. **Lotus,** for example—where one of the $80,000 treasures is said to be stashed—was known as Marshall in 1849, in honor of James Wilson Marshall of Sutter Mill fame. In 1850 the settlement became known as Uniontown, a name that commemorated California's admission to the Union in that year as the nation's 31st state. Years later, when the post office arrived on the scene, the community was assigned the name Lotus (because of a second Uniontown in Humboldt County, which is now known as Arcata). The tiny town has been known as Lotus ever since. It is located approximately a mile and a half downriver from the famous gold discovery site.

To find **Bloody Run,** where $40,000 is thought to be buried, it will be even more important to have a good map. In fact, an early map of Nevada County would probably be the best, as many new maps don't even show it. Located in rough country, the remains of this aged mining camp lie in a northwesterly direction from Nevada City. The site is accessible only over unimproved (and seldom used) roads. If you plan to go, be sure to get permission from the proper authorities, and, as in any off-road expedition, don't trespass on private property, and be sure to leave things as you found them for others to enjoy.

While I'm passing out advice, I might add that if you finally find your "pot of gold," be sure to think twice before you discard or break the container the treasure is in. For example, the pickle bottles that held the treasure of **Old Man Hawkins** are quite collectable in their own right!

An interesting detail about **Joseph F. A. Marr** and his trove of 50-dollar gold slugs is the story of where the slugs came from. Unknown to many (including some old-timers) is information indicating that they were minted in Mariposa County's private Mount Ophir Mint (one of several early California mints).

Incidentally, the slugs reportedly were buried somewhere around the settlement of Agua Fria, possibly near Marr's house. Today a marker near Agua Fria Creek (about six miles east of Mariposa) shows where the town once stood. In case you happen to visit the site and stumble across a cache of coins, I should mention that the 50-dollar slugs will be easy to identify, as they are hexagonal (six-sided) in shape.

If you do make it to Agua Fria, you might want to stop for a moment and think about the past. Even though there isn't much more than a historical marker to indicate the spot, in the town's boom days (1850–1851) Agua Fria was the seat of Mariposa County. While this may not seem like much, back then Mariposa County took in land that now is distributed among 10 other counties. In fact, Mariposa County made up approximately one sixth of the entire state of California!

Two of the stories in Chapter 7 involve **African Americans** who spent part of their lives as slaves. Although it is sad that some gold seekers from southern states were able to bring slaves to California, the freewheeling atmosphere of the gold camps did make it harder to keep men and women in bondage. In fact, the word was spread among African Americans on the East Coast and elsewhere that the California gold fields were one place where all comers counted just the same, regardless of race or religion. As a result, many freeborn African Americans joined in the rush for gold—and for equality.

Unfortunately, like the lure of instant riches, the promise of equal treatment often led to cruel disappointments. The gold camps had their share of prejudice and discrimination, not only against blacks but also against Chinese, California Indians, and Spanish-speaking people, among others. Nevertheless, a number of African Americans did manage to make a new start during the Gold Rush.

This aspect of California history deserves greater attention, as even many history buffs are unaware of the important role played by African Americans—both slave and free—in the Gold Rush years and beyond. If you would like to explore this topic further, you might want to start with the book *Blacks in Gold Rush California,* by Rudolph M. Lapp, which is a useful reference for teachers. For the experiences of other groups, see Clifford E. Trafzer's *California's Indians and the Gold Rush* (written for young readers) and F. D. Calhoon's *Coolies, Kanakas, and Cousin Jacks* (an informal book for adults that discusses no fewer than 14 ethnic groups).

One of those who got a new lease on life during the Gold Rush was **Buster,** the former slave who reportedly buried gold and coins worth $50,000 in the vicinity of Camp San Antone.

One source suggests that the treasure may have ended up in the hands of a friend of Buster's who took care of him during his last illness. This possibility, coupled with the fact that Camp San Antone is now a "ghost camp" on privately owned land, has stopped most treasure hunters from seeking Buster's cache.

In discussing **Stoddard and the lake of gold,** I indicate that there is some question about Stoddard's first name. Various accounts call him Robert, Thomas, and J. R. Other sources credit the discovery of the lake to someone else altogether. Some of the names they mention are Thomas Ballard, Caleb Greenwood, Francis Lingard, and Adam Lingaard.

Questions also remain about what happened to Stoddard after he slipped away from the expedition. I indicate in the text that he wasn't seen again in the Gold Country, and this version of the tale certainly makes sense. However, some sources say that he *was* seen again and that he even tried to organize a second expedition to search for the elusive lake. Incidentally, a popular publication that discusses the Plumas County area where Stoddard made his getaway states that it became known as Humbug Valley, as it was there that his "humbuggery" became known.

Even though the golden lake eluded discovery, for some the hunt turned out to be a profitable adventure. According to one respected source, three prospectors from Germany made an unexpected strike as they were returning to their camp from the "Gold Lake" fiasco. Upon crossing the North Fork of the Feather River (quite a distance from where the expedition began), they reportedly found particles of gold lodged in the cracks and crevices of several rocks. Settling right down to work, the excited threesome turned up $36,000 worth of gold in just four days!

As with many "accidental" finds, the Germans' strike started a rush to the region and opened up the area to mining. A number of other argonauts who arrived on the scene also staked valuable claims, and in this way profited indirectly from the ill-fated search for the lake of gold.

Of course, if there really was a Gold Lake, it was probably known to the area's Indians long before Stoddard or any other outsider visited the Sierras. There is even a story that may bear this out. After James Marshall's famous discovery, local Indians told Sutter about a lake that was situated far back in the mountains, among towering cliffs. The Indians said the lake contained vast quantities of gold. They added that it was home to a monster so terrifying that they refused to go there!

It seems appropriate that I end on this note of myth and mystery, for there are few events as fabled as the California Gold Rush. I hope that this small treasure trove of tales has whetted your appetite for even more exploration of one of the most exciting and colorful chapters in the history of our Golden State.

SELECTED INDEX
(People and Places)

ABOUT THE AUTHOR

Randall A. Reinstedt was born and raised on California's beautiful and historic Monterey Peninsula. After traveling widely throughout the world, he spent fifteen years teaching elementary school students, with special emphasis on California and local history. Today he continues to share his love of California's beauty and lore with young and old alike through his immensely popular publications. Among his many books is **More Than Memories: History & Happenings of the Monterey Peninsula,** an acclaimed history text for fourth-graders that is used in schools throughout the Monterey area.

Randy lives with his wife, Debbie, in a house overlooking the Pacific Ocean. In addition to his writing projects, he is in great demand as a lecturer on regional history to school and adult groups, and he frequently gives workshops for teachers on making history come alive in the classroom.

ABOUT THE ILLUSTRATOR

A native Californian, Ed Greco has spent most of his professional career as a graphic designer and illustrator. Born and raised in the Santa Clara Valley, Ed grew up studying and illustrating northern California, its environment, and its history.

Randall A. Reinstedt's
History & Happenings of California Series

Through colorful tales drawn from the rich store of California lore, this series introduces young readers to the historical heritage of California and the West. "Author's Notes" at the end of each volume provide information about the people, places, and events encountered in the text. Whether read for enjoyment or for learning, the books in this series bring the drama and adventure of yesterday to the young people of today.

Currently available in both hardcover and softcover:

Lean John, California's Horseback Hero

One-Eyed Charley, the California Whip

Otters, Octopuses, and Odd Creatures of the Deep

Stagecoach Santa

The Strange Case of the Ghosts of the Robert Louis Stevenson House

Tales and Treasures of California's Missions

Tales and Treasures of California's Ranchos

Tales and Treasures of the California Gold Rush

Hands-On History *teacher resource books are available to accompany titles in the* **History & Happenings of California Series***. Packed with projects and activities integrating skills across the curriculum, these imaginative resource books help bring California history to life in the classroom.*

For information about the **History & Happenings of California Series***, as well as other titles by Randy Reinstedt for both children and adults, please write:*

GHOST TOWN PUBLICATIONS
P. O. Drawer 5998
Carmel, CA 93921

112